World Book's Documenting History
Federation of Australia

WORLD BOOK

a Scott Fetzer company
Chicago

www.worldbookonline.com

World Book, Inc.
233 N. Michigan Avenue
Chicago, IL 60601
U.S.A.

For information about other World Book publications, visit our Web site at **http://www.worldbookonline.com** or call **1-800-WORLDBK (967-5325).**

For information about sales to schools and libraries, call **1-800-975-3250 (United States)**, or **1-800-837-5365 (Canada).**

© 2011 World Book, Inc. All rights reserved. This volume may not be reproduced in whole or in part in any form without prior written permission from the publisher.

WORLD BOOK and the GLOBE DEVICE are registered trademarks or trademarks of World Book, Inc.

Library of Congress Cataloging-in-Publication Data
Federation of Australia.
    p. cm. -- (World Book's documenting history)
   Includes bibliographical references and index.
   Summary: "A history of the settlement and founding of Australia, based on primary source documents and other historical artifacts. Features include period art works and photographs; excerpts from literary works, letters, speeches, broadcasts, and diaries; summary boxes; a timeline; maps; and a list of additional resources"-- Provided by publisher.
   ISBN 978-0-7166-1504-0
   1. Australia--History--Juvenile literature. 2. Australia--History--Sources--Juvenile literature. 3. Australia--Politics and government --Juvenile literature. I. World Book, Inc. .
   DU110.F43 2011
   994--dc22
                                        2010021332

World Book's Documenting History
Set ISBN 978-0-7166-1498-2
Printed in Malaysia by TWP Sdn Bhd, JohorBahru
1st printing September 2010

Staff

Executive Committee
Vice President and Chief Financial Officer
  Donald D. Keller
Vice President and Editor in Chief
  Paul A. Kobasa
Vice President, Licensing & Business Development
  Richard Flower
Chief Technology Officer
  Tim Hardy
Managing Director, International
  Benjamin Hinton
Director, Human Resources
  Bev Ecker

Editorial
Associate Director, Supplementary Publications
  Scott Thomas
Senior Editors
  Shawn Brennan
  Kristina Vaicikonis
(Manager, Contracts & Compliance
(Rights & Permissions)
  Loranne K. Shields

Manager, Research, Supplementary Publications
  Cheryl Graham
Editorial Researcher
  Jon Wills
Administrative Assistant
  Ethel Matthews

Editorial Administration
Director, Systems and Projects
  Tony Tills
Senior Manager, Publishing Operations
  Timothy Falk
Associate Manager, Publishing Operations
  Audrey Casey

Graphics and Design
Manager
  Tom Evans
Coordinator, Design Development and Production
  Brenda B. Tropinski
Senior Designer
  Isaiah W. Sheppard, Jr.
Associate Designer
  Matt Carrington

Production
Director, Manufacturing and Pre-Press
  Carma Fazio
Manufacturing Manager
  Steven K. Hueppchen
Production/Technology Manager
  Anne Fritzinger
Production Specialist
  Curley Hunter
Proofreader
  Emilie Schrage

Marketing
Associate Director, School and Library Marketing
  Jennifer Parello

Produced for World Book by
Arcturus Publishing Limited

Writer: Nathaniel Harris
Editors: Cath Senker, Alex Woolf
Designer: Jane Hawkins
Photo Researcher: Shelley Noronha

Contents

Arrival in Australia 4-5
Free Settlers 6-7
Aborigines and European Settlers 8-9
The Gold Rush 10-11
The Eureka Stockade 12-13
New South Wales and Tasmania 14-15
Victoria and South Australia 16-17
Queensland and Western Australia 18-19
Linking the Colonies 20-21
The Crisis of the 1890's 22-23
Australian Nationalism 24-25
The Federal Idea 26-27
The Federal Council 28-29
Sir Henry Parkes 30-31
The 1890 Conference 32-33
What Form of Federation? 34-35
The First Federal Convention 36-37
The People's Conventions 38-39
New Zealand Stays Out 40-41
The Second Federal Convention 42-43
The Referendums 44-45
The United Kingdom Approves 46-47
The Birth of a Nation 48-49
The First National Elections 50-51
The New Parliament 52-53
Sir Edmund Barton 54-55
Voting Rights for Women 56-57
A New Capital 58-59
Timeline 60
Sources 61
Additional resources 62
Index 63-64

Arrival in Australia

THE FIRST SETTLERS IN AUSTRALIA were the ancestors of present-day Aborigines, the first people of Australia. They arrived at least 50,000 years ago. In 1770, the English Captain James Cook (1728-1779) sailed up the eastern coast of Australia, which he named New South Wales and claimed for Great Britain. On Jan. 26, 1788, a British fleet landed the first European settlers in Sydney Cove. The settlers were not volunteers, but about 750 convicts. Over the next few years, more fleets arrived carrying prisoners. Convict labor built Sydney—later Australia's biggest city—and other early settlements. Conditions were harsh, but many convicts prospered, and most stayed on in Australia.

1

Besides *corporal* [physical] punishment to the extent of 50 to 75 lashes, and even, in some rare instances, 100 lashes, solitary confinement, and months, or even years, of hard labour in chains (on the roads or at a penal settlement) are *lightly* [easily] ordered for crimes in themselves of no *deep dye* [great importance]; petty thefts, . . . drunkenness, *insolence* [rudeness to superiors], disobedience, desertion, quarrelling among themselves, and so forth.

Alexander Maconochie

◀ The Scottish reformer Alexander Maconochie (1787-1860) describes the treatment of convicts on the island of Tasmania in a report published in the United Kingdom in 1838. The treatment of convicts in the Australian colonies grew harsher beginning in the 1820's, as their numbers increased. Conditions were particularly bad in Tasmania, which eventually held the largest convict population. More than 160,000 prisoners were sent from Britain to Australia between 1788 and 1868, when *transportation* (sending convicts to serve their sentences abroad) finally ended.

▼ A chain gang in Hobart Town, Tasmania, in about 1831. Chain gangs of convicts labored in such open-air public works as road building and clearing land. These convicts were generally men regarded as hardened or dangerous criminals. They were closely guarded. Each convict had chains around his ankles and had to hold up the end of his chain to walk. Chains made it difficult for prisoners to run away or to launch a mass attack on their guards.

2

Arrival in Australia

▶ A song, sung by convicts in Australia around 1825-1830, describes what happened when free settlers arrived and began farming. Convicts were sent to work for the settlers and were often treated like slaves or even beasts of burden and forced to pull plows. Van Diemen's Land was an earlier name for Tasmania.

> The first day that we landed upon the fatal shore,
>
> The settlers came around us full twenty score or more;
>
> They ranked us up like horses and they sold us out of hand
>
> And they yoked us up to ploughing frames to plough Van Diemen's Land.
>
> **Convicts' song**

◀ A convict's woolen work jacket issued by the British government to Tasmanian convicts in the 1850's. It is similar in style to British Army jackets of the period except for some small official markings. Convicts were no longer shipped to Tasmania after 1853, but for years afterward the island held many aging convicts until they completed their sentences.

NOW YOU KNOW

- The first European settlers in Australia were convicts sent from Britain in 1788.
- By 1868, more than 160,000 convicts had been transported to Australia.
- Convict labor was vitally important in building early modern Australia.

Free Settlers

In 1788, the first free settlers in the Australian colonies were people in charge of convicts, such as officials and soldiers, and their families. Free immigrants began to arrive in 1793. Many more came from 1831 onward, when the British government offered financial help. Free land and convict labor were strong attractions, and sheep farming became a major industry as explorers opened up large grassland areas. New settlements grew up around the coasts of the continent, and the future capitals of the Australian states were founded—Sydney, Hobart, Brisbane, Perth, Melbourne, and Adelaide. By 1850, there were around 430,000 European or European-descended people in Australia.

▶ In a 1788 letter, British Major Robert Ross (1740-1794), lieutenant governor of the new colony of New South Wales, tries to convince the British undersecretary for the colonies to abandon the attempt at settlement. Ross was a troublemaker, but he was not exaggerating. The rocks, swamps, and sand dunes of Sydney Cove almost defeated the colonists. They were close to starvation for the first two years, relying on supplies from Britain. In the early 1790's, the settlers began to master their new environment.

1

I do not scruple [hesitate] to pronounce that in the whole world there is not a worse country than what we have yet seen of this. All that is contiguous [near] to us is so very barren and forbidding that it may with truth be said that here nature is reversed... for almost all the seed we have put into the ground has rotted.
Robert Ross, 1788

2

We enjoy here one of the finest climates in the world.... The necessaries of life are abundant, and a fruitful soil affords us many luxuries.... landscape; almonds, It is now spring, and the eye is delighted with the most beautiful... landscape—almonds, apricots, pear, and apple trees are in full bloom, the native shrubs are also in full flower, and the whole country gives a grateful perfume.
Elizabeth Macarthur, 1795

◀ In September 1795, British settler Elizabeth Macarthur (1766-1850) writes enthusiastically to a British friend about the climate and soil of New South Wales, unaware that many other parts of the continent were less favored. Elizabeth was also one of the lucky settlers. Her husband, John Macarthur (1767-1834), became one of the most powerful men in the colony. His position as an army officer enabled him to acquire a very large farm just outside Parramatta, with wheat fields, an orchard, and a thousand sheep, where he and Elizabeth lived in style.

Free Settlers

3

▲ A painting of Parramatta in 1820 makes the settlement look like a romantic English landscape. Parramatta was founded by the first governor of New South Wales, Arthur Phillip (1738-1814), who intended its pleasant, regular layout to outshine the sprawling town of Sydney. However, it was Sydney that grew into a great city and became the capital of New South Wales.

NOW YOU KNOW

- In 1788, officials and soldiers and their families became Australia's first free settlers.
- Free immigrants arrived beginning in 1793 and in greater numbers beginning in 1831.
- By 1850, coastal and inland settlements had grown, and the settler and convict population was around 430,000.

Aborigines and European Settlers

ABORIGINES HAD LIVED IN AUSTRALIA for more than 50,000 years before the Europeans arrived. Aborigines were divided into clans and tribes speaking about 250 languages, with about 600 dialects. They were skillful hunters, fishermen, and food-gatherers with a *nomadic* (wandering) way of life. Each tribe had its own territory and sacred places. Europeans thought of Aborigines as primitive people without governments or systems of land ownership. Britain claimed Australia and settlers bought or occupied land without recognizing Aboriginal rights. As the settlers' holdings expanded, conflicts with the Aborigines became increasingly violent. The Aborigines were weakened by European diseases and outgunned by the settlers. Aboriginal numbers fell rapidly, and by the late 1800's they were a poor, badly treated minority.

1

> We are at war with them: they look upon us as enemies—as invaders—as oppressors and persecutors—they resist our invasion. They have never been *subdued* [put down by force], therefore they are not rebellious subjects, but an injured nation, defending, in their own way, their rightful possessions which have been torn from them by force.
>
> *Launceston Advertiser*, 1831

◀ The writer of an 1831 letter to a Tasmanian newspaper defends the Aborigines' right to resist the European invaders who were stealing their land and destroying their way of life. Many European settlers, however, believed that the only way they could settle the country was to terrify the Aborigines with violence.

2

▶ An 1834 portrait of the severed head of Yagan (1795?-1833), a famous Aboriginal warrior. Yagan was captured in 1832 after he led an attack in which an immigrant laborer was killed. Yagan was held on an island and made a daring escape by boat. He was described as a striking figure, and many Europeans admitted that they admired him. In 1833, he was involved in a raid and declared an outlaw. Yagan was shot for the reward by a herder.

Aborigines and European Settlers

3

> They came, sad remnant of a bygone race,
> Surviving mourners of a nation dead: . . .
> They came like straggling leaves together blown,
> The last memorial of the *foliage* [leaves] past;
> The living bough upon the tree o'erthrown,
> When branch and trunk lie dead.
>
>   Hobartia

◀ A poem published in 1834 in the *Hobart Town Magazine* describes the plight of the Tasmanian Aborigines. In the 1830's, the small number who survived were shipped away, allowed to return only in old age. The anonymous poet (pen name "Hobartia") recognized that the Tasmanian Aborigines had been treated unjustly, but clearly believed that they were doomed members of "a bygone race" whose history was over. According to one estimate, the Aboriginal population in Australia had shrunk from about 600,000 in 1821 to fewer than 300,000 in 1850. The decline went on into the 1900's, but the Aboriginal people did survive.

4

▶ A newspaper illustration from around 1860 depicts spear-wielding Aborigines attacking a shepherds' hut in Tasmania. The shepherds are armed with rifles, but they are outnumbered. Such pictures reflected settlers' anger at Aboriginal tactics, which were most often a form of *guerrilla* (sudden raid) warfare. The Europeans' overwhelming advantage in firepower, and massacres of Aborigines, were less well publicized.

NOW YOU KNOW

- The Aborigines had lived for thousands of years in Australia when Europeans arrived there.
- Europeans occupied more and more land in Australia, which led to conflicts with the Aborigines.
- Europeans defeated the Aborigines, whose population declined steeply.

The Gold Rush

In April 1851, prospector John Lister and his partners discovered gold near Bathurst, New South Wales. Shortly afterward, there were new and much bigger finds in the neighboring colony, Victoria. The result was the Australian gold rush. Prospectors raced to the gold fields from all over Australia and other parts of the world. Within a few years, the country was transformed. The non-Aboriginal population rose from 430,000 in 1851 to 1.15 million in 1861. The country's new wealth helped expand its cities, encouraged manufacturing, and paid for large imports of goods. It launched an era of prosperity and national self-confidence.

▶ In his 1882 book *Reminiscences of an Adventurous and Chequered Career at Home and at the Antipodes*, South Australian police commissioner Alexander Tolmer (1815-1890) describes gold prospectors at work in 1852. As a law enforcer he was probably disturbed by the gathering of so many "uncouth-looking" men and the policing problems that fierce competition for riches were likely to cause.

1

Let the reader imagine thousands of bearded, *uncouth* [rough]-looking men, dressed in dirty short *jumpers* [jackets], with trousers the colour of yellow ochre, busily at work—some filling carts with gold-*impregnated* [filled] earth, and carting it to the bank of the creek, lined with cradles, where washers were in full operation.

Alexander Tolmer, 1882

◀ An 1851 color print by the British naturalist and painter George French Angas (1822-1886) depicts gold washing in Summerhill Creek at Ophir, Bathurst, soon after the gold rush began. Ophir was the first area where gold was found. It was named after a place of great wealth mentioned in the Bible. The picture is romanticized, with a handful of prospectors and unspoiled natural surroundings. There would actually have been hundreds of people at this place, along with tents, tools, and a large quantity of litter.

The Gold Rush

3

Let men, for instance, avoid all sorts of fancy waistcoats, dandy boots, or costly cravats and ties; let women *shun* [turn away from] the idle vanities of silks and satins, of lace and ribbons, of many flounces and fashionable bonnets; and let both men and women forget that there are such things in the world as *kid* [leather] gloves, lavender water and toilet tables.

John Capper, 1855

◀ In his book *The Emigrant's Guide to Australia*, published in 1855, John Capper supplies would-be prospectors and their wives with travel information, maps, and practical advice. Capper lists the luxuries that immigrants would have to give up, though it seems unlikely that people bound for the gold fields would have been used to living in such style.

▶ The washing cradle was a device used by prospectors to separate gold from other materials. Earth and water were shoveled into the cradle, which had a metal sieve inside. The heavy gold fell onto a tray in the cradle, while the earth and water were washed away. The cradle was introduced in Australia by the British prospector Edward Hargraves (1816-1891). He had seen similar models used during the 1849 California gold rush.

4

NOW YOU KNOW

- In 1851, discoveries of gold in New South Wales and Victoria triggered a gold rush by prospectors throughout Australia and from other countries.
- Australia's new wealth from gold attracted settlers and stimulated the growth of manufacturing.
- Australia's non-Aboriginal population more than doubled between 1851 and 1861

The Eureka Stockade

During the gold rush, miners in Ballarat, Victoria, clashed violently with local officials. The miners complained about the expensive licenses they had to buy and about their lack of political and other rights. When government troops arrived in the area, the miners prepared to resist, building a *stockade* (wooden fortification) at Eureka. On Dec. 3, 1854, troops captured the stockade, killing about 30 miners. When miners were put on trial for *treason* (betraying their own country), juries refused to convict them. The miners quickly achieved most of their aims, and the Eureka Stockade became a symbol of a new, democratic-minded Australia.

1

NOTICE.

Government Camp, Ballarat, Dec. 3rd, 1854.

Her Majesty's forces were this morning fired upon by a large body of evil-disposed persons of various nations, who had entrenched themselves in a stockade on the Eureka, and some officers and men killed.

Several of the rioters have paid the penalty of their crime, and a large number are in custody.

All well-disposed persons are earnestly requested to return to their ordinary occupations, and to *abstain* [refrain] from assembling in large groups, and every protection will be afforded to them by the authorities.

      ROBT. REDE, Resident Commissioner.
      God save the Queen.

◀ The police commissioner's notice states the government's case against the rebellious miners. Some historians have argued that, whatever the miners' complaints, the government had to act against the threat of rebellion.

2

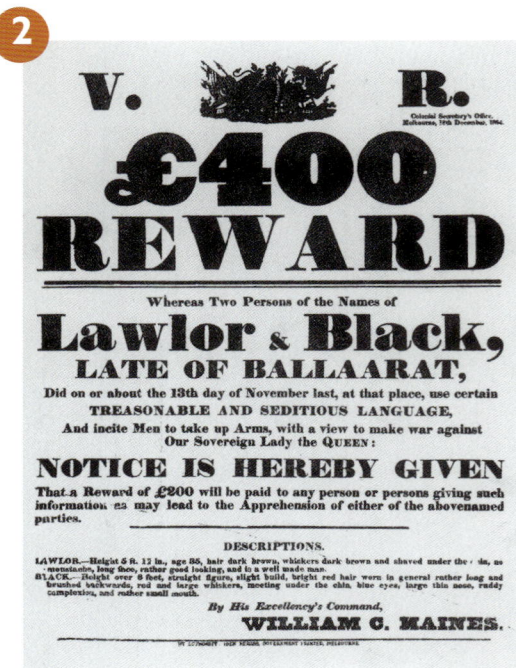

▶ An 1854 poster offers a reward of 400 pounds for information leading to the arrest of Peter Lalor (1827-1889; here spelled Lawlor) and George Black, leaders of the miners who fought at the Eureka Stockade. Lalor was the fieriest of the miners' leaders. As a popular hero, he was later elected to the parliament of Victoria and had a successful political career.

The Eureka Stockade

▶ An 1854 newspaper report describes the fighting at the Eureka Stockade. It explains how the troops continued to attack miners who could not defend themselves or were trying to surrender. Such accounts helped to strengthen public sympathy for the miners.

> Some men were killed outright, others dangerously wounded, and a few slightly hurt from shots and sword marks from the troopers, who after the fight was all over and all resistance passed by, kept up firing at such unfortunates as presented themselves from the doorways of tents to see what was going on.
>
> *Geelong Advertiser*, Dec. 4, 1854

◀ A homemade battle flag flown by the defiant Eureka miners. The miners swore on it that they would stand together against the government. The stars on the flag are arranged roughly in the shape of the Southern Cross, a *constellation* (group of stars) mainly visible from south of the equator. The Southern Cross came to symbolize Australia and appears on the present-day Australian flag.

NOW YOU KNOW

- In 1854, Ballarat miners protested the cost of licenses to dig for gold and demanded political and other rights.
- In December 1854, the miners built the Eureka Stockade, which was attacked by government forces.
- The Australian public supported the miners, and the Eureka Stockade came to be seen as an important step in the development of Australian democracy.

New South Wales and Tasmania

NEW SOUTH WALES WAS THE FIRST AUSTRALIAN COLONY, founded in 1788. The settlers developed farming, sheep raising, and whaling industries. The colony was further enriched by the 1851 gold rush. It became self-governing in 1856. Originally, all the British settlements in Australia were part of New South Wales. As more distant areas developed, they were organized as separate colonies. The second colony was the island of Tasmania (Van Diemen's Land until 1856). Convicts arrived beginning in 1803. Free settlers arrived beginning in 1804, and the capital of Hobart was settled that same year. Tasmania separated from New South Wales on Dec. 3, 1825, and by 1856, it too was fully self-governing.

▶ The New South Wales Constitution Act of 1855 lays down who may vote in elections for the new Legislative Assembly. All the members of the new Assembly were to be elected. (Before the act, some members had been government appointed). Only men who owned property worth 100 British pounds could vote. At the time, it was widely believed that property owners alone should be entitled to vote. After 1858, all adult men in New South Wales, Victoria, Tasmania, and South Australia could vote for their Assemblies.

> The Qualifications for Electors of the Legislative Assembly shall be as follows:—
> Every Man of the Age of Twenty one Years, being a natural born or naturalized Subject of Her Majesty, or legally made a *Denizen* [citizen] of New South Wales, and having a *Freehold Estate* [property owned outright] in possession, situate in the District for which his Vote is to be given, of the clear Value of One hundred Pounds *Sterling* [British] Money....
>
> from the New South Wales Constitution Act of 1855

◀ The first elected government of New South Wales, 1856. The colony's first *premier* (head of government) was Stuart Donaldson (1812-1867) (center). Also shown, *left to right,* are Colonial Treasurer Thomas Holt (1811-1888), Attorney General William Manning (1811-1895), Solicitor General John Bayley Darvall (1809-1883), and Auditor General and Secretary for Lands and Works George Nichols (1809-1857).

New South Wales and Tasmania

3

> When I landed at Hobart Town . . . the population of the island amounted to about 66,000: of these 29,000 were convicts . . . In spite, however, of this . . . life and property were as secure, I may indeed say with truth more secure, than in England: there were no shutters to the windows, no locks to the doors. . . . I do not of course mean that the population was unusually virtuous or orderly; but there was an active and efficient police . . . consisting nearly altogether of convicts; [and] there was an admirable system of rewards and punishments. . . .
>
> — Sir William Denison, 1870

◀ Sir William Denison (1804-1871) describes his first impressions of Tasmania, where he served as lieutenant governor from 1847 to 1855, in his 1870 autobiography, *Varieties of Vice-Regal Life*. According to Denison, almost half the population were convicts, but the colony was rapidly settling down. A convict police force kept crime well under control.

▼ A group of Tasmanian schoolboys pose with their master, the English-born poet and clergyman James Hebblethwaite (1857-1921) (bearded man at right), at Buckland's Private School in Hobart around 1894. The school had up to 70 students and provided a general education to boys 7 years and older.

4

NOW YOU KNOW

- All of the early settlements in Australia were part of the first colony, New South Wales.
- As new areas of Australia developed, they became separate colonies.
- Tasmania became a colony in 1825 and achieved full self-government in 1856.

Victoria and South Australia

Successful settlement in Victoria began in 1834, and Melbourne, its capital, was founded in 1835. On July 1, 1851, Victoria became a separate colony from New South Wales, and the gold rush of that year made it very wealthy and heavily populated. In 1856, Victoria became self-governing. South Australia was first colonized in 1836 by free settlers who founded its future capital, Adelaide. It was the only Australian colony that never admitted convicts transported from Britain. After a slow beginning, South Australia prospered, helped by discoveries in the 1840's of copper deposits that encouraged immigration by creating jobs. It too became self-governing in 1856.

1

> There shall be established in Victoria, instead of the Legislative Council now *subsisting* [that now exists], One Legislative Council and One Legislative Assembly, to be . . . *constituted* [established] in the Manner *herein-after* [afterwards] provided; and Her Majesty shall have Power, by and with the Advice and Consent of the said Council and Assembly, to make Laws in and for Victoria, in all Cases whatsoever.
>
> from the Victoria Constitution Act of 1855

◀ The Victoria Constitution Act of 1855 made the colony self-governing. The Legislative Council and Legislative Assembly were Victoria's two law-making bodies. A premier—like a prime minister in Britain—headed the colony's government. He could stay in office only while he was supported by the lawmaking bodies. This arrangement was described as "responsible government." Britain kept control of such matters as the colony's relations with foreign powers.

2

▶ A watercolor sketch by the British-born artist William Strutt (1825-1915) records the opening of the new Parliament of Victoria in November 1856. Strutt was a notable colonial artist who recorded many events of his day. He was also a successful portrait painter.

Victoria and South Australia

▶ A letter published in an 1833 newspaper expresses high hopes for the future settlement of South Australia. The settlements were based on careful plans put forward by the British colonial reformer Edward Gibbon Wakefield (1796-1862). Immigrants would receive help to pay for their passage to Australia, but would have to buy their land and work hard. In the 1800's, many people believed that work and *virtue* (goodness) were closely linked. This belief led the letter writer to conclude that a *virtuous* (good) South Australia would benefit orphaned children.

The new colony of South Australia offers *peculiar* [special] facilities for the employment and protection of orphan and *destitute* [very poor] children. The climate is *salubrious* [healthful], and the arrangements . . . will surround the children with an industrious population. . . . The population of the new colony, consisting entirely of voluntary emigrants, will, it is hoped, be a virtuous community, and thus be desirous of *ministering* [doing helpful things], not only to the outward comforts of the children, apprenticed in the colony, but to their moral culture and improvement.

The Perth Gazette and Western Australian Journal,
July 20, 1833

◀ Members of South Australia's Legislative Assembly debate in the House in this 1867 painting by the Scottish-born artist James Shaw (1815-1881).

NOW YOU KNOW

- Victoria was made wealthy by the gold rush and became a separate colony in 1851.
- South Australia was the only colony that never had convict settlements.
- Both Victoria and South Australia became self-governing in 1856.

Queensland and Western Australia

THE MOST HARDENED CONVICTS of New South Wales were sent in 1824 to settle the area that became Queensland. In 1839, the convicts were replaced by free settlers. On June 6, 1859, Queensland became self-governing. With a varied climate, Queensland had large areas of grazing land but also produced sugar cane. Beginning in 1867, it benefited from gold strikes. Western Australia was founded by free settlers in 1829, but with its vast desert areas and small population, the colony failed to make progress. In 1850, the British government sent convicts, selected for their skills and good behavior, to work in the colony. Western Australia became the sixth and last of the self-governing Australian colonies on Oct. 21, 1890.

▶ In sending New Year greetings to its readers in 1859, the Brisbane newspaper *The Moreton Bay Courier* focuses on separation from New South Wales. At that time, Queensland was still part of New South Wales and was ruled from the capital of Sydney. Many Queenslanders believed the remote government was little concerned with their interests. In June 1859, Queensland became not only a separate colony but also self-governing.

The past year was great in promises that the next march of time would give us Separation [from New South Wales]. We have looked for the time so long, that we shall be greatly disappointed if 1859 deceives us. . . . A Happy New Year—and [here's to] Separation from Sydney mismanagement.

The Moreton Bay Courier, Jan. 1, 1859

Every person of the age of twenty-one years . . . who shall have resided in Western Australia for six months, shall . . . be entitled to be registered as an elector. . . . No aboriginal native of Australia, Asia or Africa, or person of the half-blood, shall be entitled to be registered, except in respect of a *freehold qualification* [unless they are property owners].

Constitution Acts Amendment Act, 1899

◀ An 1899 act gave the vote to all adults in Western Australia, including women. (South Australia had become the first colony to grant women the right to vote, in 1894.) Aborigines and other nonwhite people were not allowed to vote unless they owned property. The amendment reflects the strong racist attitudes that led to the mistreatment of Aborigines and later the White Australia policy designed to prevent non-Europeans from settling in Australia (see pages 24-25).

Queensland and Western Australia

▲ Parliament House in Brisbane, Queensland, when it opened in 1868. When Queensland became a separate colony in 1859, Brisbane had a population of about 5,000. The Legislative Assembly met for the first time in 1860 in the Old Convict Barracks, chosen because it was one of the capital's largest buildings at the time. The new Parliament House was designed by the British-born colonial architect, Charles Tiffin (1833-1873), who was inspired by the Louvre in Paris.

NOW YOU KNOW

- Western Australia was founded by free settlers but later needed convict labor to progress to self-government in 1890.
- Queensland's varied climate made it suitable for grazing and also for growing sugar cane.
- By 1890, Australia had been divided into six separate, self-governing colonies.

Linking the Colonies

AFTER 1850, THE AUSTRALIAN COLONIES BECAME VERY PROSPEROUS. Sheep raising and farming expanded. Gold mining created great wealth. Deposits of silver, lead, copper, and coal were also found. Cities grew rapidly, and by the 1880's the Australian population approached 3 million. The telegraph—and, above all, railroads—began to draw the distant colonies together. During the 1880's, railroad construction rapidly increased. However, each colony created its own railroad system, which did not match its neighbors' systems. Passengers and freight had to transfer to a different train at the border between colonies. Such issues suggested that Australia needed a central government authority.

1

> Everyone who has taken any interest in the history of railroad works in this colony during the last few years, must remember the rather fierce controversy which took place during the progress of legislation on . . . the comparative merits of the system of construction adopted in the United States of America and that known as the British system, now adopted all over Europe.
>
> *The Argus*, Jan. 5, 1859

◀ A letter published in the 1859 Melbourne *Argus* reveals that there were arguments over railroad systems in Victoria in the 1850's. The main issue was which *gauge* the colony should adopt. A gauge is the distance between the rails on which the train wheels run. The gauge determines the distance between a locomotive's wheels and, therefore, its overall design. Although a debate took place in Victoria, the decisions of other colonies were ignored, partly through a short-sighted belief that travel between colonies would never be of much importance.

2

▶ An 1891 illustration depicts a train steaming down the Zig Zag Railway through the Blue Mountains of New South Wales. The line's "zig-zag" route and three sandstone *viaducts* (railroad bridges) are visible. These and the two tunnels represented a feat of engineering in mountain country.

Linking the Colonies

▶ In this photograph taken in 1900, a locomotive pulls logs out of the Geeveston Forest in Tasmania's Southern Region. Logging was a major island industry, at first carried out by convict labor in terrible conditions. By the time of federation in 1901, all states except Western Australia were linked by rail, with more than 12,000 miles (20,000 kilometers) of track.

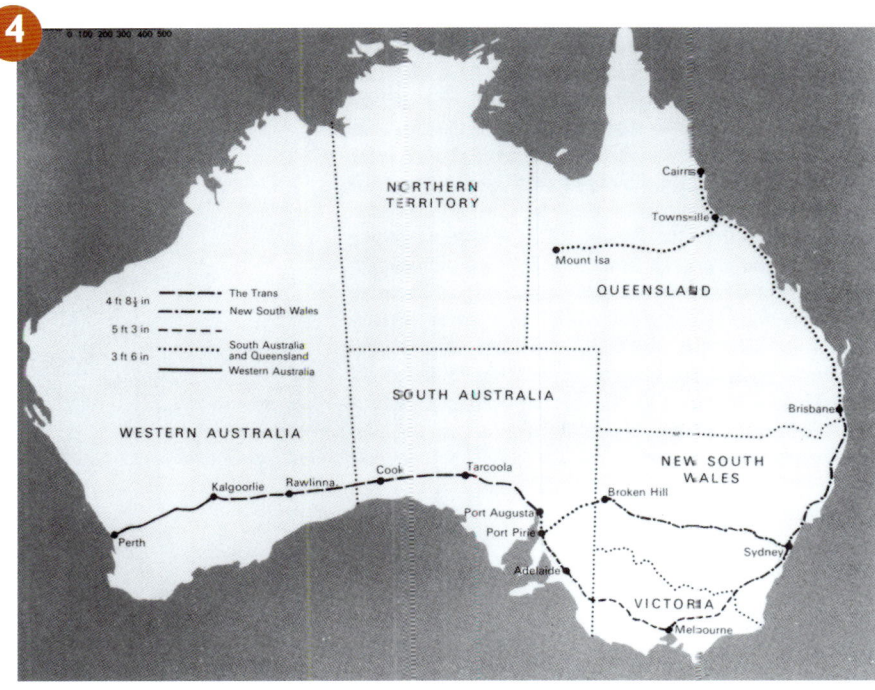

◀ A map of Australia's railroads in 1917 shows that there were no railroad lines across huge areas of the interior, emphasizing that the main population centers were all close to the coasts. The nation's first north-south railroad was completed in 2004. It extends from Adelaide in South Australia to Darwin in the Northern Territory.

NOW YOU KNOW

- Australia enjoyed great prosperity after 1850.
- Telegraph and railroads linked the six colonies.
- Each colony created its own railroad system, making no attempt to fit the systems smoothly together.

The Crisis of the 1890's

AUSTRALIA'S LONG *BOOM* (PROSPEROUS TIME) ended in the 1890's. Individuals and colonial governments had borrowed heavily, and banks had lent money freely. When the good times ended, the colonies found themselves in trouble. Governments employed fewer people, and unemployment rose steeply. Banks forced borrowers to repay their loans, causing hardship. The banks also suffered when people withdrew money from their accounts. In 1893, the entire banking system nearly collapsed. Conflicts between employers and trade unions added to the sense of crisis. Some people thought that a national Australian government might have dealt with the problems more successfully.

▲ An 1889 illustration depicts members of the Eight-Hour Day Movement taking part in a procession in Melbourne. In 1856, men in the Melbourne building trade had won the right to work an eight-hour day. From 1850 to 1890, many other groups established their right to an eight-hour day. The success of the movement encouraged later efforts of workers to band together to protect or advance their interests.

▶ A letter published in the October issue of the Melbourne journal *Table Talk* shows that some people realized in 1891 that banks were lending recklessly. By 1893, many were forced to close. The crisis was worst in Melbourne, the center of the Australian financial system. The bank crashes exposed scandals involving unfair or dishonest practices. As a result, many savers lost confidence in the banks and rushed to take out their money, worsening the situation.

> Let their *books* [bank records] be examined, and what will be found? Loans on land, loans on houses erected by *speculative* [risk-taking] builders: in fact loans to everybody except the persons who really could and would like to develop the country if they had an opportunity. . . .
>
> *Table Talk*, 1891

The Crisis of the 1890's

3

> He *exhorted* [urged] all unionists to hold well together and fight the battle stubbornly out to the end, always being careful . . . to remain strictly within the law. He explained that . . . the Amalgamated Shearers' Union was endeavouring to . . . come to an *amicable* [friendly] settlement of terms . . . but if . . . no satisfactory terms could be arrived at, he called upon all shearers to simply refuse to go to work; let them all unitedly stand out.
>
> *The Brisbane Courier*, June 3, 1891

◀ *The Brisbane Courier* reported this speech by a local leader of the Amalgamated Shearers' Union during a national shearers' strike that began in Queensland in 1891. Many other trade unions went on strike in Australia in the early 1890's. Employers, aided by government troops and police, broke the strikes. Many trade unionists then turned to political action, leading to the creation of the Australian Labor Party, which still exists.

4

◀ A cartoon depicts *depositors* (people with bank accounts) at Melbourne's Union Bank lining up to withdraw their money during Australia's 1893 bank crisis. If depositors panic and all want to withdraw their money, a bank may be unable to pay and will then have to go out of business.

NOW YOU KNOW

- In the early 1890's, Australia's long boom ended and there was an economic crisis.
- The Australian banking system came close to collapse, and unfair financial practices were discovered.
- During the early 1890's, many workers went on strike but governments and employers defeated them.

Australian Nationalism

By the 1880's, Australians had a strong sense of being one people, living in a single nation. By this time, a majority of Australians were native-born. Most Australians had British ancestors, and most remained conscious of being members of the British Empire. Yet shared experiences, such as the gold rush, had created a distinctive Australian outlook. It had a strong emphasis on equality, expressed in movements such as trade unionism and the new Labor Party. However, Australian hostility toward Chinese and other non-European immigrants led to anti-Chinese riots, restrictions on immigration, and in the 1900's, the White Australia policy.

1

> Unarmed, defenceless and unresisting Chinese were struck down in the most brutal manner by bludgeons provided for the occasion, and by pick handles. . . . Some of the acts of barbarism said to have been committed here were such, that Englishmen can scarce be brought to *credit* [believe] that their countrymen could be guilty of them. . . .
>
> *The Sydney Morning Herald*, July 20, 1861

◀ The writer of this newspaper article angrily reports on an anti-Chinese riot that took place in Lambing Flat, New South Wales, on June 30, 1861. It was the most serious of a series of gold-field riots against Chinese miners that started in the 1850's. Around 2,000 miners attacked and injured Chinese workers, destroying most of their belongings. The report refers to "Englishmen" when it clearly means fellow Australians, suggesting a strong emotional attachment to the mother country.

▶ A cloth banner carried by miners during the 1861 riot at Lambing Flat. The painted Southern Cross design was intended to appeal to the spirit of the Eureka Stockade (see pages 12-13), but was directed against foreigners (Chinese immigrants) rather than the government.

Australian Nationalism

◀ Soldiers *subdue* (overcome) anti-Chinese protesters in an illustration depicting the Lambing Flat riot. The artist clearly sympathizes with the rioters, depicting them as victims. In reality, government action to restore order usually came too late, and it was the Chinese who suffered. Feeling against Chinese immigration was so strong that all the Australian colonial governments passed laws against it.

▶ The writer of an 1890 newspaper *editorial* (article giving the newspaper's view) sides with working people in their disputes with employers over conditions of labor. According to the writer, economists on the employers' side portrayed workers as needing to be tired out by long hours of labor to stop them from falling into "intemperate" habits such as drunkenness. The writer insists that shorter hours of labor would make workers more productive.

Such so-called economists *allege* [argue] that the highest good is *conferred upon* [given to] the working man when he is so fully engaged in labouring, eating, and sleeping as to leave him no time to plot against his employer, [or] to acquire *intemperate* [bad] habits. But this allegation is a *libel* [untrue statement] upon the working classes. . . . There can be no question that the results of shortened hours of labour mean better work, an improved educational and moral tone among the industrial classes, and a higher scale of comfort for their families.

The Brisbane Courier, March 1, 1890

NOW YOU KNOW

- By the 1880's, Australians had begun to feel that they were one people, though still closely linked with Britain.
- By the 1880's, the majority of people in the country had been born there.
- There was widespread hostility toward Chinese and other non-European immigrants.

The Federal Idea

The Australian colonies grew up separately, divided by great distances. They valued their independence, and *rivalries* (competition) between them led to separate railroad systems, defense forces, and *tariffs* (taxes on imports and exports) between colonies. The idea of uniting through some form of federation began to gain support only in the 1880's, as Australian nationalism emerged. In a federation, separate units, such as colonies or states, join together to create a central government. The federal government's powers are limited, and the colonies or states retain important rights and duties. In Australia, federation would prove hard to achieve.

1

Until the three or four young colonies become more advanced in population, wealth and social progress, and get experience in the working of their separate political institutions, is it not very probable that the attempt to form a general assembly [all-colonies meeting] will embroil the whole of them in discord [conflict] and dissatisfaction with each other and with the Parent State [Britain]?

George Fife Angas, 1849

◀ Letter written by George Fife Angas (1789-1879), one of the founders of South Australia, to Henry George Grey (1802-1894), the third Earl Grey, in 1849. As the *colonial secretary* (person in charge of all British colonies), Grey proposed that the Australian colonies should send delegates to meet and work together over differences such as tariffs. Angas's opposition to a delegates' meeting or "general assembly" was widely supported by Australians, and Grey dropped the scheme.

▶ In a widely publicized speech by Sir Henry Parkes (1815-1896) (see pages 30-31) at Tenterfield, New South Wales, on Oct. 24, 1889, the politician argues against the view that there were not enough Australians to form a government spanning the continent. He points out that Australia then had roughly the same population as the American colonies did in 1781, when they won their independence from Britain. If the Americans could do it, he asserts, so could the Australians.

2

The great question they had to consider was whether the time had not now arisen for the creation on this Australian continent of an Australian government. . . . Australia had now a population of three and a half millions, and the American people numbered only between three and four millions when they formed the great commonwealth of the United States. The numbers are about the same, and surely what the Americans had done by war, the Australians could bring about in peace.

The Sydney Morning Herald, Oct. 25, 1889

The Federal Idea

▶ Passage from an 1889 report by British military expert Major General James Bevan Edwards (1835–1922). Edwards recommends a federation of the armed forces of the Australian colonies. To many of the colonial leaders, it seemed vital that the Australian colonies speak with a united voice in their own foreign affairs and have the capacity to defend themselves as a nation. Parkes used Edwards's findings to support a call for wide political federation in his Tenterfield speech.

> Looking . . . to the fact that it is the unforeseen which happens in war, the defence forces should at once be placed on a proper footing; but this is, however, quite impossible without a federation of the forces of the different colonies.
>
> Major General James Bevan Edwards

▲ The *Cerberus*, shown here in 1904, was a powerful, up-to-date battleship when it was launched in 1868. Ordered by the government of Victoria, it became the colony's flagship. Although some British warships were stationed in Australia, each of the colonies also had its own naval defense force. The idea of a single Australian navy provided a strong argument for federation. The *Cerberus* remained in service until 1924.

NOW YOU KNOW

- The Australian colonies developed separately and were not enthusiastic about working together.
- In the 1880's, nationalist feeling grew stronger, making the idea of federation more appealing.
- In 1889, Sir Henry Parkes campaigned for the federation of Australia.

The Federal Council

IN 1883, DEFENSE ISSUES seemed likely to set the colonies on the road to federation. French and German activity in the Southwest Pacific alarmed all the British colonies in the region. That year, the colonies planned a Federal Council of Australasia (Australia, New Zealand, and other Southwest Pacific territories). The council first met in 1886, without New Zealand, South Australia, or New South Wales. Fiji dropped out in 1888; South Australia in 1891. New South Wales never joined the council. Already weakened, the council had little real power. It could pass laws but it could not enforce them. The Federal Council stopped meeting after 1899. The council achieved little, but it did encourage several colonies to work together.

1

> The Japanese, after a sleep of 2000 years, are rousing themselves and looking ahead.... The French in New Caledonia are also thinking beyond the day, while *Prussia* [Germany], Russia, and France are looking eagerly at New Guinea and other islands near our coasts. With the whole East seething and boiling with awakening energy, and with threats of war and rumors of war, it would be criminal if we continue asleep, and, as portions of the British nation, do not consider the importance of defending ourselves against foreign attack. To do this there must be federation.
>
> *The Brisbane Courier*, Jan. 19, 1876

◀ *The Brisbane Courier* reports a statement by South Australian Premier James Boucaut (1831-1916). Boucaut, an early supporter of federalism, makes a direct link between defense needs and federal union. Like most federalists, Boucaut was not aiming to separate Australia and Britain, but rather saw the colonies as "portions of the British nation."

2

> Sir George Turner said the discussion clearly showed the uselessness of the Federal Council. As long as it did not contain representatives of all the colonies it would be absurd to pass an Act of the Federal Council which was to come into operation or remain in operation at the sweet will and pleasure of New South Wales.
>
> *The Sydney Morning Herald*, Jan. 28, 1899

▶ A newspaper reports some frank remarks made by Sir George Turner (1851-1916), the premier of Victoria, as he presided over a meeting of the Federal Council. The Federal Council was able to do little unless New South Wales—a nonmember—was prepared to back its decisions.

The Federal Council

▼ The representatives of four Australian colonies and other staff pose for a photograph at the final meeting of the Federal Council in 1899. The first four figures from the left in the front row are the colonial premiers John Forrest (1847-1918), Western Australia; James Robert Dickson (1832-1901), Queensland; Sir George Turner, Victoria; and Sir Edward Braddon (1829-1904), Tasmania.

NOW YOU KNOW

- Fears of German and French expansion in the Southwest Pacific region led to the creation of the Federal Council of Australasia.
- The council was weakened by the absence of several states and its limited powers.
- The council's last meeting was in 1899.

Sir Henry Parkes

Sir Henry Parkes has been called "the father of federation" for his role in urging the six separate British colonies on the Australian continent to combine to form the Commonwealth of Australia. Born in England, he immigrated with his family to New South Wales in 1839. Parkes became a businessman and journalist before going into politics in 1854. He served as premier of New South Wales five times between 1872 and 1891. On Oct. 24, 1889, Parkes's call at Tenterfield for urgent talks on federation (see pages 26-27) made an immediate impact. He was an impressive but controversial figure, often accused of being a crafty deal maker rather than a man of principle. Parkes campaigned for a federated Australia until his death in 1896.

1

First and foremost of course in every eye was the commanding figure of Sir Henry Parkes, than whom no actor ever more carefully posed for effect. His huge figure, slow step, deliberate glance and carefully brushed-out *aureole* [halo] of white hair combined to present the spectator with a *picturesque* [quaint] whole which was not *detracted from* [lessened] on closer acquaintance.

Alfred Deakin,
The Federal Story

▲ In his book *The Federal Story,* Victoria politician Alfred Deakin (1856-1919) recalls Parkes at the age of 75 at the 1890 conference in Melbourne.

2

▶ Parkes's forceful personality is captured in a striking photograph from the 1880's.

Sir Henry Parkes

▶ A Melbourne newspaper portrays Parkes as a glory seeker, unwilling to help the Federal Council because he could not run it. *The Argus* was not *unbiased* (without prejudice), since it represented opinion in Victoria, the great rival of New South Wales.

Circumstances had prevented Sir Henry Parkes from acquiring the management of the Federal Council, and he could not bring himself to co-operate with that body. He had determined to outvoice and outbid the men who had been trying to help forward the cause of federation against the *apathy* [lack of activity] of New South Wales, and *hence* [therefore] he suddenly appeared before the world with a vague scheme for a ... Parliament. According to Sir Henry Parkes, Australia is ripe for federation.

The Argus, Jan. 1, 1890

◀ In a 1900 cartoon by Sydney cartoonist H. Cotton (1872-1931), Parkes unveils a federated Australia. Parkes did not live to see his dream of federation come true.

NOW YOU KNOW

- British-born Sir Henry Parkes was five times premier of New South Wales.
- Parkes became known as Australia's "father of federation."
- Parkes died before the Commonwealth of Australia was formed in 1901.

The 1890 Conference

TO BRING ABOUT FEDERATION, Parkes wanted to hold an intercolonial convention of delegates from all the colonies to prepare a constitution. The premiers of the other colonies responded cautiously. A preliminary conference of leading figures from the Australian colonies and New Zealand was held in Melbourne from Feb. 6 to Feb. 14, 1890. Despite some disputes, the week-long conference in Melbourne went well. The colonies selected delegates for a National Australasian Convention to be held in Sydney in 1891. The members resolved on "early union under the Crown" and agreed to draw up a constitution for a federal Australia at the convention.

▶ In a speech at the 1890 conference, Sir Samuel Griffith (1845-1920), premier of Queensland, outlines the basic issue very clearly. The colonies differed widely in population, importance, and opinions. Were they ready for a "perfect" federation or would limited links be more suitable?

1

I apprehend we are met here principally for the purpose of exchange of ideas amongst ourselves, as representing the public opinions of the different colonies, as to how far Federation is practicable [able to be done] at the present time.... Some members of the Conference believe that a perfect [complete] Federation is possible now, others that it is not practicable, and they may feel it their duty to point out the difficulties. And those difficulties will have to be met.

Sir Samuel Griffith, 1890

2

The first and most pressing reason given for [federation] is the necessity of organizing the military defences of Australia. The arguments set forth by Sir Henry Parkes on this subject ... appear to me quite irresistible. To think that Australian military forces, organized by five or six different Governments, paid by five or six different Governments, acting under the authority of five or six different Governments, can equal in efficiency ... the same number of men belonging to one Government ... is, I think, the merest dream.

Sir John Hall, 1890

◀ In a speech at the conference, Sir John Hall (1824-1907), the New Zealand representative, points out the advantages of a common defense effort. In agitating for federation, Parkes emphasized defense issues, taking advantage of an 1889 British report on Australian weaknesses in that area (see page 27). The advantage of a single defense policy became a powerful argument for federation. Even some federation opponents, including Hall, favored organizing a single Australian defense force.

The 1890 Conference

▲ An illustration in the British newspaper *The Graphic* depicts the 1890 conference in session. Not all of the leaders at the conference are in the picture. From left to right (on bench) are Hall and William Russell (1838-1913) representing New Zealand; William McMillan (1850-1926) representing New South Wales; John Alexander Cockburn (1850-1929) and Thomas Playford (1837-1915) representing South Australia; and Deakin representing Victoria. Parkes, representing New South Wales, is at the table at the left, with G. H. Jenkins, conference secretary, at the far end. Duncan Gillies (1834-1903), representing Victoria, is in the background. Andrew Inglis Clark (1848-1907), representing Tasmania, stands right.

NOW YOU KNOW

- Parkes agreed to a preliminary conference of leading figures from the Australian colonies and New Zealand.
- At the 1890 conference, the advantages of a single defense policy were seen as a powerful argument for federation.
- The conference agreed to hold a convention to draw up a federal constitution.

What Form of Federation?

THE 1890 CONFERENCE DECIDED THAT THE TIME WAS RIGHT for the colonies to federate. Yet there was no final decision about which form of federation should be written into the constitution. There were several existing systems that were discussed as possible models. The Swiss Confederation gave the central government only limited powers. In contrast, Canada's federal government was strong. The most favored model was the form of national government established by the Constitution of the United States, with its careful balance and separation of federal and state powers. The details of Australia's constitution would be decided at the 1891 convention. Behind the scenes, drafting of a constitution for Australia began almost at once.

◀ The U.S. Constitution was the most favored model for Australia's new constitution. Its *preamble* (introductory statement) and seven articles were written in 1787. Delegates to the Constitutional Convention signed the document in Philadelphia on September 17. It was *ratified* (approved) in 1788. The first page of this famous document is shown here.

What Form of Federation?

2

... it seems to me that the founding of the United States affords us this one warning against anything short of a complete Constitution. We know that after the struggle for independence the United States tried to live under ... the Articles of Confederation ... but year by year they grew weaker, more dissatisfied, more incapable of attending to the real wants of even one of the States, and ... nothing could follow ... but disaster, ruin, and acquisition [takeover] by a foreign Power. It was only the failure of this system which compelled the states at last to accept the Constitution under which they have lived and thriven [succeeded]. ...

Sir Henry Parkes, 1890

▶ A passage from an editorial in the Melbourne *Argus* newspaper highlights the long process that would have to occur to achieve federation. The road to federation turned out to be even longer.

◀ At the 1890 conference, Parkes speaks in favor of an Australasian federation with an active central government. He argues his case using an example from American history during the last years of the Revolutionary War (1775-1783). Beginning in 1781, the 13 American states were loosely linked by the Articles of Confederation, with a central legislature but no central government. The Articles were blamed for U.S. problems in the 1780's. The U.S. Constitution of 1787, which created a federal government, was believed to have transformed the country's fortunes.

3

It is possible ... that the clock has struck the hour for a Federal Parliament but even if everything goes smoothly much time will be taken in *instituting* [setting up] the new system. The various Parliaments will have to appoint delegates to a convention officially charged with the task of preparing a constitution; that constitution must be submitted to the *various* [colonial] Parliaments for their *ratification* [approval]; and an act will then have to be passed by the Imperial *Legislature* [British Parliament]. Even if no hitch occurs three, four, or five years may easily roll by before the end is attained. ...

The Argus, Feb. 8, 1890

NOW YOU KNOW

- The 1890 conference agreed on federation, but not on which form it should take.
- The conference considered Swiss, Canadian, and U.S. forms of federation as models.
- The U.S. form of federation was the most favored.

The First Federal Convention

THE NATIONAL AUSTRALASIAN CONVENTION was held from March 2 to April 9, 1891, in Sydney. Delegates from the six Australian colonies and New Zealand were present. In 1890, Andrew Inglis Clark had privately written a *draft* (proposed) constitution for a federated Australia. With revisions by Sir Samuel Griffith and others, the draft was accepted by the convention. The colonial parliaments seemed certain to approve it. But the New South Wales parliament delayed; Parkes became ill and resigned his premiership in late 1891. The process stalled and discussions in other colonies petered out. Throughout Australia, the colonial governments were facing the effects of economic depression. Industrial disputes and financial hardships in the colonies drew more concern than federation.

1

> Unless where it is otherwise expressed or implied this Act shall commence and have effect on and from the day so appointed in the Queen's proclamation; and the name "The Commonwealth of Australia" or "The Commonwealth" shall be taken to mean the Commonwealth of Australia.
>
> from Australia constitution draft, 1890

◀ In this passage from a draft of the Australia constitution, Clark refers to the proposed Australian federation as "The Commonwealth of Australia." When federation was achieved, this name was adopted. Many other parts of Clark's draft also appeared in the 1901 Australian constitution. The many American-inspired features in the draft included a legislature consisting of two bodies: a House of Representatives elected on the basis of population and a Senate in which each *state* (former colony) would have the same number of members. The scheme was modified by the introduction of British features, such as a government headed by a prime minister.

▼ Members of the 1891 Australasian Federation Convention. Parkes stands center.

2

The First Federal Convention

▶ These principles, which were put forward at the beginning of the convention, describe the basic operation of the proposed federation. The second statement meant that Victoria would have to give up its policy of imposing high tariffs on goods from other colonies. The statement of principles was followed by resolutions outlining the federal Parliament, government, and legal system. There were long and often angry arguments that eventually ended in *compromise agreements* (settlements where both sides give up something). Finally, all the delegations approved a draft constitution to be presented to the colonial parliaments.

3

That . . . the principles embodied in the Resolutions following be agreed to:--

(1.) That the powers and privileges and territorial rights of the . . . existing Colonies shall remain intact, except . . . such surrenders as may be agreed upon as necessary . . . to the power and authority of the National Federal Government.

(2.) That the trade and *intercourse* [relations] between the Federated Colonies . . . shall be absolutely free

(3.) That the power and authority to impose Customs *duties* [taxes on goods] shall be exclusively lodged in the Federal Government and Parliament. . . .

(4.) That the Military and Naval Defence of Australia shall be entrusted to Federal Forces, under one command.

Principles of federation, 1891

4

Our cause is the consolidation of Australian interests. Each colony . . . will be as she ever was, but . . . the . . . colonies united will have a power they can only obtain by federation, and that power alone will give them a proper place in the family of nations. I ask you then, with unreserved feeling, with true hearts, earnestly engaged in this great work to drink this toast: One people. One destiny.

Sir Henry Parkes, 1891

◀ Henry Parkes made a toast at a banquet to mark the opening of the 1891 National Australasian Convention on March 2. In the toast, he used the phrase "One people, one destiny," which became a famous slogan for the Australian federation movement.

NOW YOU KNOW

- Delegates from the six Australian colonies and New Zealand took part in the Australasian Federal Convention.
- A draft constitution was accepted by the delegates for approval by the colonies' parliaments.
- In the late 1890's, industrial disputes and financial hardships in the colonies drew more concern than federation.

The People's Conventions

POLITICIANS DEBATED FEDERATION, but most Australians showed little interest. Public attitudes began to change in the 1890's. *Federal leagues* (profederation societies) spread through the colonies. Many people began to feel that a united Australia was needed to tackle the then-current economic depression. A well-known politician, Edmund Barton (1849-1920) (see pages 42, 50-51, 54-55), campaigned vigorously for federation. From July 31 to Aug. 1, 1893, an unofficial "People's Convention" was held in Corowa, New South Wales. At the convention, John Quick (1852-1932), an English-born lawyer, argued for a national convention to which delegates would be elected by popular vote from each colony. It produced a new program of action, taken up in 1895 by a meeting of premiers at Hobart. In 1896, a second People's Convention, at Bathurst, kept up the pressure for political action.

◀ Portrait of John Quick, 1898. Quick, one of the founding fathers of federation in Australia, played a leading role at the Corowa People's Convention in 1893. Quick was also a delegate at the National Australasian Convention in 1897-1898 that further advanced the federation movement (see pages 42-43).

▶ As a newspaper report indicates, the key proposal at the Corowa convention was a resolution introduced by Quick that was enthusiastically received. Quick's proposal had two new, democratic features: (1) Representatives to a new federation convention were to be elected, not appointed. (2) Each colony was to agree or disagree with the proposed constitution through a *referendum* (vote by all the people) rather than a vote by each colonial parliament.

Dr. Quick introduced the following motion . . . "That in the opinion of this conference the legislature of each Australasian colony should pass an Act providing for the election of representatives to a . . . convention or congress to consider and adopt a bill to establish a federal constitution for Australia and upon the adoption of such bill or measure it be submitted by some process of referendum to the verdict of each colony."

. . . The resolution received general approval. That portion dealing with the referendum was specially *commended* [praised]. It was finally carried with cheers and enthusiasm.

The Sydney Morning Herald, Aug. 2, 1893

The People's Conventions

▶ A report on the convention from the same edition of *The Sydney Morning Herald* observes politician John Chanter's (1845-1931) call for the people to move the federation forward. Chanter established the Australian Natives' Association in New South Wales. The Corowa convention was mainly organized by the Australian Natives' Association and the Australasian Federation League. Chanter worked closely with the leading profederalist, Barton.

> Mr. Chanter . . . stated that . . . No doubt the various parliaments were greatly to blame for the present state of things. The only remedy was for the people to take the matter in hand.
>
> *The Sydney Morning Herald*, Aug. 2, 1893

SCHOOL OF ARTS.

▲ A drawing from the 1890's shows the School of Arts at Bathurst, New South Wales, where the second People's Convention was held in 1896. Although an unofficial gathering, the convention was attended by such leading figures as George Reid (1845-1918), the premier of New South Wales.

NOW YOU KNOW

- In the 1890's, interest in federation grew, and federal leagues spread through the colonies.
- In 1893, the People's Convention at Corowa proposed new, more democratic procedures for deciding the federation issue.
- The colonial premiers took up the Corowa proposals in 1895 in Hobart, and a People's Convention in Bathurst in 1896 pressed for further action.

New Zealand Stays Out

NEW ZEALAND SENT DELEGATES to the 1890 conference and the 1891 convention. But the New Zealanders' doubts grew as it became clear that the Australian colonies favored a strong federal government. Such a government would inevitably be mainly Australian and located in Australia. New Zealand, about 1,000 miles (1,600 kilometers) away, was unlikely to have much influence on government decisions, but would have to obey them. New Zealanders were also uneasy about other issues such as tariffs and voting systems. After 1891, New Zealand took no active part in the federation movement, and hopes that it would join later on came to nothing.

1

... I think I am dealing justly with the whole of the people in proposing that if they desire to have this constitution at all, every man who pleases may vote upon that question upon the principle of one man one vote. I feel certain that if that is not acceded [agreed] to, the probability is that the people of New Zealand will absolutely reject the constitution.

Sir George Grey, 1891

◀ At the 1891 debates of the National Australasian Convention, Sir George Grey (1812-1898), the New Zealand representative, objects strongly to the practice in some Australian colonies of plural voting, which gave wealthy people more than one vote. He insists that an Australasian constitution should be decided on the principle of "one man one vote." Eventually plural voting was abolished, but by then there was no question of New Zealand joining the federation.

▶ A cartoon from the September 1899 issue of *The New Zealand Graphic* reveals that the idea of federating with the Australian colonies was still alive. In the cartoon, federation is "in the air" and New Zealand is depicted as a small boy riding on the tail of a kangaroo, symbolizing Australia. The statement that New Zealand, if partnered with Australia, would progress by "leaps and bounds" is jokingly based on the kangaroo's jumping movement.

2

FEDERATION IN THE AIR.
ONE POSSIBLE VIEW OF THE POSITION OF NEW ZEALAND.

New Zealand Stays Out

▶ The act that created the Commonwealth of Australia, passed by the Parliament of the United Kingdom, identifies New Zealand as a state with an automatic right to enter the Australian Commonwealth. This is striking evidence that New Zealand's membership was still regarded as desirable and likely.

3

... whereas it is *expedient* [advantageous] to provide for the admission into the Commonwealth of other Australasian Colonies and possessions of the Queen: "The States" shall mean such of the colonies of New South Wales, New Zealand, Queensland, Tasmania, Victoria, Western Australia, and South Australia ... as for the time being are parts of the Commonwealth, and such colonies or territories as may be admitted into or established by the Commonwealth as States.

from the Commonwealth of Australia Constitution Act, 1900

◀ A 1900 cartoon, also from *The New Zealand Graphic*, depicts New Zealand as a noble young woman resisting the advances of an ogre (the Australian Federation) because his "arms bear chains," that is, they would make a slave of New Zealand.

NOW YOU KNOW

- New Zealand took part in the 1890 conference and the 1891 convention to establish an Australasian federation.
- New Zealand was uneasy with the Australian colonies' desire to create a strong federal government.
- Fearing that it would have little influence on such a government, New Zealand took no further part in the federation movement.

The Second Federal Convention

In 1895, the colonial premiers met in Hobart and agreed that delegates should be directly elected to a new constitutional convention. Each colony had to pass an *enabling act* to make this possible. An enabling act is a law that authorizes individuals or groups to do things they would otherwise have no power to do. From 1895 to 1896, New South Wales, Victoria, South Australia, and Tasmania passed the acts. Western Australia's parliament took a different course, appointing delegates. Queensland did not pass an enabling act and was not represented at the convention. The convention was held in three sessions in Adelaide, Sydney, and Melbourne between March 1897 and March 1898. The final draft of the constitution was still based on the 1891 constitution, with changes mainly in a more democratic direction. The next, decisive step would be to hold referendums.

1

> It is to be hoped that the feelings of the majority of your readers . . . have been *quickened* [stirred] to a lively sense of the injury they suffer as citizens of Queensland at the hands of Sir Hugh Nelson and the government of this colony. It seems evident that Queensland will ultimately for its own benefit have to federate with the other colonies . . . the question of election of delegates . . . to represent Queensland has been allowed to drop out of sight. The affair of the election was strangled in its *inception* [beginning] by the action of Sir Hugh Nelson, which will not soon be forgotten. . . .
>
> *The Brisbane Courier*, March 8, 1897

◀ In a letter to *The Brisbane Courier*, an angry Queenslander complains that the government of Sir Hugh Nelson (1835-1906) prevented Queenslanders from taking part in elections to the convention. The situation in Queensland was complicated by severe divisions within the colony that led to a breakaway attempt by the northern region.

▼ Delegates at the first session of the 1897 federal convention in Adelaide. The president, Charles Kingston (1850-1908), premier of South Australia, sits in the center of the front row. Also present are other premiers and Barton, official leader of the convention and chief drafter of the constitution.

2

The Second Federal Convention

3

There are many people in these colonies who look upon this Constitution from a conservative point of view. They think that it is far too democratic. They point out that in no Constitution which has yet existed in the world have there been two Houses of Legislature in which property has no representation at all.

Sir Richard Baker,
Melbourne, 1898

◀ South Australian delegate Sir Richard Baker (1842-1911) defends the democratic tendencies in the draft constitution at the 1898 convention in Melbourne. He points out that even in countries where all adult men had the vote, one of the two lawmaking bodies represented the wealthier section of society, supposedly in the interests of stability. The 1898 draft constitution particularly angered conservatives by proposing that Australia's future Senate should be elected, not appointed.

▼ A souvenir poster of the Australasian Federal Convention (Second Federal Convention) was issued by the government of Victoria in 1898. The poster includes a list of delegates, a picture of the houses of Parliament in Melbourne, and portraits of the five colonial premiers (clockwise from upper right): Braddon (Tasmania), Turner (Victoria), Kingston (South Australia), Reid (New South Wales), and Forrest (Western Australia).

4

NOW YOU KNOW

- New South Wales, Victoria, South Australia, Tasmania, and Western Australia sent delegates to the 1897-1898 convention.
- Queensland did not take part.
- A draft constitution was drawn up, based on the 1891 draft.

The Referendums

From June 3 to June 4, 1898, four colonies held referendums on the Commonwealth Bill containing the draft federal constitution. Neither Queensland nor Western Australia took part. Victoria, Tasmania, and South Australia registered strong "Yes" votes. In New South Wales, a majority also supported the bill, but the votes in favor, 72,000, fell short of the minimum of 80,000 needed. A second campaign was followed by new referendums between April and September 1899, with Queensland taking part. All five colonies voted in favor of the bill. At the last moment, on July 31, 1900, Western Australia also held a referendum, which returned a strong "Yes" vote.

1

Mr. Lyne spoke in terms of *unqualified* [complete] disapproval of the leading principles of the bill. His greatest objection was to the equal representation of the *states* [the former colonies] in the Senate. He said it was absolutely *antagonistic* [opposed] to the principles of pure democracy . . . that the minority of people in any two or three states combined should be able to outvote the representatives of a more populous state.

The West Australian, April 14, 1898

◀ A newspaper report describes a speech by leading New South Wales politician William Lyne (1844-1913). Lyne objected that, in the Senate, several states with small populations would be able to outvote a state with more inhabitants than all of its opponents combined. The counterargument was that equal representation in the Senate protected the small states from domination by their larger neighbors.

▶ A leaflet warns that staying out of the federation could be dangerous. Colonies inside the federation would trade freely with one another. If it was not part of the federation, a colony such as South Australia, with a small population, would be shut out and lose trade and income.

2

If the larger Colonies federate without us, we shall be powerless against such a combination which may ruin our trade and manufactures and *diminish* [lessen] our *revenues* [income]. . . . Vote "Yes" for the Commonwealth Bill on June 4th, and Advance Australia.

Commonwealth League leaflet, 1898

The Referendums

▶ A cartoon in the Sydney *Daily Telegraph* urges a "No" vote in the 1899 referendum. New South Wales, depicted as a woman, guards all her advantages (piled up behind her) against the octopuslike tentacles of federation. Many people in New South Wales, a large and wealthy colony, feared that it would be outvoted in a federation and have to pay too large a share of the costs.

◀ A record board shows the state of the vote during Western Australia's 1900 referendum. The colony had only been self-governing since 1890. It was reluctant to give up its independence so soon, especially since a gold rush had enriched it. Attitudes changed as the other five colonies moved toward federation. Western Australia finally voted for federation when delegates from the other colonies were already in London arranging for the creation of the Commonwealth.

NOW YOU KNOW

- In 1898, voters in New South Wales, Victoria, Tasmania, and South Australia voted for federation, but the referendum was lost because the number of "Yes" votes in New South Wales was too small.
- In 1899, five colonies, including Queensland, held referendums and approved the bill to create a federal Australia.
- In 1900, Western Australia held a referendum and joined the movement toward federation at the last moment.

The United Kingdom Approves

In March 1900, delegates from the colonies arrived in London for talks with the United Kingdom's colonial secretary, Joseph Chamberlain (1836-1914). Australian troops were helping the British in the Anglo-Boer War (1899-1902), and the delegates were warmly welcomed. During the talks, Chamberlain argued for changes to the bill, but the Australians ably defended it. In July 1900, the Parliament of the United Kingdom passed the Commonwealth of Australia Constitutional Bill almost unaltered. The bill then received the approval of the monarch of the United Kingdom, Queen Victoria (1819-1901). The Duke of York (1865-1936), later King George V, proclaimed the Commonwealth of Australia on Jan. 1, 1901. It would remain part of the British Empire, with the government of the United Kingdom controlling Australian foreign policy. But in most respects, Australians would now be in charge of their own destinies.

1

◀ Queen Victoria in 1897, at the time of her Diamond Jubilee (60th anniversary as queen). As well as being the monarch of the United Kingdom, Victoria was the head of the British Empire, which at that time included India, Canada, Australia, New Zealand, and large parts of Africa.

▶ Deakin contrasts Queen Victoria during her 1887 reception of the Australian delegates with her 1900 reception of the delegates. In 1900, the queen was 81 years old and failing in health. She died Jan. 22, 1901, three weeks after the birth of the Australian Commonwealth.

2

She received the Australians sitting, her voice was low and *indistinct* [unclear], she was partially deaf, requiring to be reminded in a loud voice of who they were and her eyes were lost to sight behind large clumsy spectacles of great power but with which she could only read the largest writing. . . . She smiled upon the delegates but this time not royally as in 1887 but with the weakness and weariness of an old woman.

Alfred Deakin,
The Federal Story

The United Kingdom Approves

▶ A 1900 cartoon depicts three of the Australian delegates on their way to London, as if they were characters from the popular 1889 novel *Three Men in a Boat*, by the British author Jerome K. Jerome (1859-1927). In the novel, three men and a dog have comic adventures while boating on the Thames River in England. Here, the boaters are (left to right) delegates James Dickson, Edmund Barton, and Charles Kingston. The dog "Persuasion" is needed to convince the British government to accept all the terms of the new Australian constitution.

◀ The Royal *Assent* (agreement) to the Commonwealth of Australia Constitution Act was signed by Queen Victoria and dated July 9, 1900. The queen's assent was necessary before any bill could become law. However, this assent was automatic once a bill had been passed by the two houses of Parliament. On September 17, a royal proclamation fixed the date when the act would come into force. The Commonwealth of Australia officially came into being on Jan. 1, 1901.

NOW YOU KNOW

- In March 1900, delegates from the Australian colonies arrived in London to discuss passing the bill for an Australian constitution into British law.
- The bill was passed by the Parliament of the United Kingdom and approved by Queen Victoria.
- The Commonwealth of Australia came into being on Jan. 1, 1901.

The Birth of a Nation

On Jan. 1, 1901, the Commonwealth of Australia was born, and the constitution came into operation. The six colonies became states within the commonwealth. The House of Representatives and the Senate made laws for the new federation. A governor general assented to laws and generally represented the British monarch. The High (Supreme) Court ruled on all cases concerning the constitution. The government was led by a prime minister who held office while he was supported by a majority in the House of Representatives. On January 1, people in all the states celebrated the birth of the commonwealth with processions, illuminations, and entertainments.

▶ In her book *Thirty Years in Australia,* published in 1903, the popular British-born writer Ada Cambridge (1844-1926) recalls the excitement caused by the birth of the Australian Commonwealth.

▼ About 100,000 people celebrated the birth of the Commonwealth of Australia on Jan. 1, 1901, at ceremonies held at Centennial Park in Sydney. Australia's first governor general, Lord Hopetoun (1860-1908), took the oath of office in the pavilion at the center of the photograph. This was followed by the official proclamation of the commonwealth. The pavilion is surrounded by soldiers, a mass choir, and members of the 10,000-strong procession that had wound its way through the city.

1

On the last day of 1900 I sat at my writing window . . . the morning papers had warned us to set our time-pieces . . . so as not to be a second out, if we could help it, when the midnight hour should strike. I cannot describe . . . the sense of fateful happenings that possessed us that day. . . . Australia believed herself on the threshold of the Golden Age. I myself openly boasted of my happiness. . . .

Ada Cambridge, 1903

2

The Birth of a Nation

3

... the city was thronged as it has never been before. The public and private buildings were *profusely* [extravagantly] and tastefully decorated, and several triumphal arches had been erected.... There were three distinct processions, the first being military, the second friendly and labor societies, and the third children.... Tonight the city was flooded with light.... At the town-hall a national concert was held in the evening, and a *pyrotechnic* [fireworks] display was on Perth water, while torchlight processions paraded the streets.

The Argus, Jan. 2, 1901

◀ A report in Melbourne's *Argus* newspaper describes the celebration of the new commonwealth in Perth, the relatively small capital city of Western Australia. The enthusiasm is striking in view of the colony's last-minute decision to join the federation.

▶ Sydney's large post office building is splendidly illuminated to celebrate the creation of a united Australia. Electrification was still a relative novelty, making such a display even more impressive. Many other parts of the city were illuminated. Even reporters from Sydney's great rival, Melbourne, acknowledged "with pride and pleasure that New South Wales and her noble capital have in every respect risen to the occasion."

NOW YOU KNOW

- The colonies became states within the commonwealth on Jan. 1, 1901.
- The constitution called for the House of Representatives and the Senate to make laws and the governor general to assent to laws. The governor general represented the monarch.
- The government was led by a prime minister who was supported by a majority in the House of Representatives.

The First National Elections

ON JAN. 1, 1901, EDMUND BARTON BECAME AUSTRALIA'S FIRST PRIME MINISTER. Once in office, Barton's government scheduled federal legislative elections for March 29 and 30. Three main groups competed for power in the first elections. The Protectionist Party, led by Barton, believed in helping Australian industries by taxing foreign imports. The Free Trade Party, led by George Reid, opposed tariffs. The Labor Party was the most recently formed and, at this point, the weakest party. It stood for working people's rights. The Protectionists won most seats but not a majority. But Labor was strongly *protectionist* (supportive of import taxes) and agreed to support Barton, who formed the commonwealth's first elected government.

▲ Voters at a polling booth in Hyde Park, Sydney, 1901. Voting in Australia had been by secret *ballot* (vote) since the 1850's. In 1901, the process was undoubtedly fair, though some voters complained that the ballot papers were too complicated and the pencils provided too blunt!

The First National Elections

▶ Voting instructions published in the Adelaide *Advertiser*, 1901. South Australian voters in the federal elections were also reminded who was entitled to vote. This was necessary because each state conducted the proceedings according to its own existing laws. As a result, Aborigines could vote in four states (a right later withdrawn), while women could take part in South Australia and Western Australia.

At the polling-booth TWO VOTING PAPERS will be handed to the elector. One will give the names of the candidates for the Senate; the other those of the candidates for the House of Representatives. SIX SENATORS are to be elected, and SEVEN MEMBERS of the HOUSE OF REPRESENTATIVES.

There are eleven candidates for the Senate and seventeen for the House of Representatives. The voter must not mark crosses opposite the names of more than SIX on the SENATE voting paper, or of more than SEVEN on the HOUSE OF REPRESENTATIVES voting paper.

Mark each CROSS WITHIN THE SQUARE.

The Advertiser, March 27, 1901

We advise the electors to vote for the following candidates . . . who have spoken most plainly and consistently on the all-important question of free trade and protection. Beware of the wobblers . . . who propose to support Mr. Barton and the Victorian boss [Alfred Deakin], though they declare themselves freetraders. . . . For the Senate (6) J. S. Clemons, Jas. Macfarlane, R. C. Patterson, Hon. D. C. Urqhart, J. B. Waldron, J. B. W. Woollnough. For House of Representatives (5) Sir E. N. C. Braddon, Norman Cameron, Hon. W. Hartnoll, Hon. F. W. Piesse. The electors can choose the fifth member for themselves, as we see no candidate that we can heartily recommend.

The Mercury, March 28 1901

◀ In the run-up to the voting on March 29, the Hobart *Mercury* published a list of Tasmanian candidates it supported. At this time, political parties were very loose groupings, and only the Free Trade Party had any kind of national organization. The local situation was unclear enough for the paper to name the candidates it believed its readers should support.

NOW YOU KNOW

- Edmund Barton became Australia's first prime minister on Jan. 1, 1901.
- The government quickly arranged elections, which were contested among the Protectionist, Free Trade, and Labor parties.
- The Protectionists emerged as the largest party, and Barton formed Australia's first elected government.

The New Parliament

On May 9, 1901, the Parliament of the Australian Commonwealth was officially opened by the Duke of York (see page 46). Queen Victoria had died in January, and her son had succeeded as King Edward VII (1841-1910). The duke was the king's son, and *heir apparent* (next in line to be king). He and his wife traveled to Australia for the ceremony, which took place in the Exhibition Building in Melbourne. The duke opened Parliament and cabled messages passed between Australia and the United Kingdom. The governor general swore in the members of the Houses of Parliament. Hymns, prayers, artillery salutes, and patriotic songs completed the ceremonies.

1

His Majesty has watched with the deepest interest the social and material progress made by his people in Australia, and has seen with ... heartfelt satisfaction the completion of ... political union ... . Gentlemen of the Senate and Gentlemen of the House of Representatives, it affords me much pleasure to convey to you this message from his Majesty. I now, in his name ... declare this Parliament open.

The Duke of York, May 9, 1901

◀ The Duke of York opened Australia's Parliament with this speech, which was the centerpiece of the ceremonies. The speech took the form of a message from the king. The duke revealed that Queen Victoria had decided to send him to open the Australian parliament, and that, despite her death, the new king had ruled that the visit should still take place. The earlier part of the speech stressed royal gratitude for the colonies' help in the Anglo-Boer War. As heir apparent, the duke was to become Prince of Wales in November 1901. He later reigned as King George V (1910-1935).

2

As the sound of the guns *reverberated* [echoed] through the building, Her Royal Highness pressed an electric button, which started a message to England, announcing that the first Federal Parliament had been opened. Almost before the people had realized that the declaration which had called the Heir Apparent expressly to Australia had been made, His Royal Highness announced in a loud and clear voice that he had just received a message from his Majesty the King.

The Age, May 10, 1901

▶ Reporting the event, Melbourne's *The Age* newspaper describes the speed of cablegram communications—at the touch of a button—with awe. The presence of royalty and same-day messages from the king were exceptional and memorable events. The king cabled a brief message of good wishes. In answering, the duke noted, "Splendid and impressive ceremony, over 12,000 people in Exhibition Building."

The New Parliament

▲ Painting of the duke opening parliament by the Australian artist Tom Roberts (1356-1931), who founded Australian Impressionism. The huge painting is about 10 by 17 feet (3 by 5.2 meters) and contains 250 recognizable portraits of notable people who took part. The duke stands at the front of the platform, with his wife, the Duchess of York (1867-1953), and the governor general immediately behind him. Among the audience in the front row are the prime minister, Edmund Barton, and other ministers. Most of the people present are dressed in black, because the royal family was still in mourning for Queen Victoria. The painting was completed in 1903 and presented to King Edward VII.

NOW YOU KNOW

- The Parliament of the Commonwealth of Australia was opened on May 9, 1901.
- Queen Victoria's grandson, the Duke of York, traveled from the United Kingdom to perform the ceremony.
- The duke read out a message from his father, King Edward VII, and the duke and the king exchanged cablegrams.

Sir Edmund Barton

MANY INDIVIDUALS CHAMPIONED THE CAUSE OF FEDERATION, but Edmund Barton is generally seen as its key figure. Born in Sydney, he became a lawyer and served in the New South Wales Parliament. A devoted federalist, Barton led the movement from 1891, when he sat on the committee that drafted the constitution. Barton led the 1897-1898 convention and headed its drafting committee. In 1900, he headed the delegation to London that saw the Commonwealth Bill passed into law. Barton served as Australia's first prime minister from 1901 to September 1903. In 1903, Barton's government established the High Court of Australia. Exhausted by the campaign for federation and his responsibilities as prime minister, Barton resigned in 1903. Several days later, he was appointed as one of three judges of the High Court.

◀ Barton at about the age of 60, a decade after leaving politics to become a High Court judge. He was knighted in 1902 in recognition of his services to the Federation of Australia.

▶ Braddon, the Tasmanian premier, pays tribute to Barton on the last day of the Federal Convention at Melbourne. Barton was the official leader of the convention and also head of the three-man drafting committee that worked on the federal constitution. The committee labored at its task for a year. Though the constitution was based on the one adopted in 1891, the committee made a great many significant amendments to it, which the convention accepted.

> We have all seen with admiration the splendid way in which our leader, the honorable and learned member [Edmund Barton], has conducted the proceedings of the Convention. We must all have admired the devotion ... shown by him and by the members of the Drafting Committee. Many honorable members are possibly unaware that they [the Committee] have given hours to ... the Bill when we have been enjoying ourselves ... and it is due to their efforts that we were able to pass the Bill as early as yesterday.
>
> Sir Edward Braddon,
> March 17, 1898

Sir Edmund Barton

3

Twelve o'clock struck, and no Minister had left the Cabinet. . . . A few minutes later the Cabinet bell began to ring, messengers moved swiftly about the building, telephone bells rang, heads of departments gathered in the main corridor, and junior clerks peeped over the stairs to . . . get an inkling of what was happening below. The atmosphere was electrical. . . . The door of the Cabinet room . . . opened, and Sir Edmund Barton walked out. . . . They thought that the Prime Minister had gone up the back staircase. . . . Instead . . . he had slipped away down through the vaults and out on to Spring-Street . . . to *evade observation* [avoid being seen]. Thus the Prime Minister took leave of the Federal Public Offices.

The Argus, Sept. 25, 1903

◀ The Melbourne *Argus* presents an interesting backstairs view of Barton's resignation, announced during a Cabinet meeting. Workers in the Melbourne parliament building had obviously heard rumors that the prime minister might decide to go, though Barton seems to have made up his mind only hours before. As the report shows, political events excited people then just as they do now, and after an important decision, leading personalities sometimes preferred to avoid reporters.

▶ Opening of the first High Court of Australia, 1903. The first three judges were men who had worked hard in the federal cause. Shown left to right are Barton, Chief Justice Samuel Griffith (see pages 32, 36), and Barton's long-time friend Richard O'Connor (1851-1912).

NOW YOU KNOW

- From 1891, Edmund Barton led the campaign for a federal Australia.
- Barton was involved at each important stage in drafting the federal constitution and oversaw its passage into law.
- Barton was Australia's first prime minister, from 1901 to 1903. He then became a judge of the High Court.

Voting Rights for Women

AUSTRALIA WAS AMONG THE FIRST COUNTRIES IN THE WORLD to give women the right to vote. Women were active in demanding the vote, and from 1884 *suffrage* (right to vote) societies were founded in all the colonies. Before federation, two colonies—South Australia (1894) and Western Australia (1899)—gave women the vote. Women in South Australia and Western Australia voted in the federation referendums and in the first federal elections in 1901. On June 12, 1902, the new federal Parliament *enfranchised* (gave the right to vote to) women (but not most non-Europeans, male or female) in all the Australian states. As in other countries, Australian women found that the vote was only the start of a long journey to full equality with men.

1

> . . . we are justified in appealing to your honourable Convention to . . . frame the Federal Constitution . . . to give the women of all the colonies a voice in choosing the representatives of the Federal Parliament, so that United Australia may become a true democracy resting upon the will of the whole and not half of the people.
>
> petition of the Womanhood Suffrage League, 1897

◀ The Womanhood Suffrage League presented a *petition* (a document making a request) to the 1897 Federal Convention asking that female suffrage be written into the constitution. Campaigners for women's suffrage often made the point that there could be no true democracy if half of the people had no vote. In 1902, Australia gave women the right to vote in national elections.

▼ A 1902 cartoon by H. Cotton shows an Australian woman being toasted by the country's male political leaders. The woman is invited to share in a banquet, meaning the political life of the nation.

2

Voting Rights for Women

3

> ... had I been elected, my first and last thought would have been given to the claims of the whole people. ... But the 7,500 votes which I received left me far enough from the lucky 10. Had Mr. Kingston [South Australian premier] not asserted both publicly and privately that, if elected, I could not constitutionally take my seat, I might have done better. There were rumours even that my nomination paper would be rejected.
>
> Catherine Helen Spence, 1910

◀ Scottish-born novelist and political activist Catherine Helen Spence (1825-1910) writes in her autobiography about running for the Federal Convention in 1897. She became the first woman in Australia to seek election. In the poll to choose 10 delegates to represent South Australia at the federal convention, Spence came 22nd out of 33 candidates. No woman was elected to a state Parliament until 1921. The first woman was elected to the federal Parliament in 1941. No Aborigine was allowed to vote until 1962.

"NEW WOMEN" OF AUSTRALIA.

▶ In a photograph from around 1900, Australian women wear clothes that allow them to walk, bicycle, and move freely. From the 1880's, "the New Woman" emerged in several countries. She was well educated and insisted on being treated as an equal by men. Although a minority, such women played an important role in the suffrage movement and also campaigned on social issues.

NOW YOU KNOW

- Australia was one of the first countries in the world to give women the vote.
- South Australia gave women the right to vote in 1894; Western Australia in 1899.
- After the commonwealth was established, Australian women (but not most non-Europeans) received the vote in 1902.

A New Capital

A UNITED AUSTRALIA NEEDED A NATIONAL CAPITAL. But rivalries between the states, and between the bigger cities, made it hard to achieve agreement. The main candidates were Sydney, the oldest city, and Melbourne, at that time the largest. The solution eventually found was to build an entirely new capital city, Canberra, which would stand in territory that did not belong to any of the states. While that was being done, Melbourne served from 1901 as the temporary capital of Australia. Building the new city took a very long time. But in 1927, the federal Parliament finally moved to Canberra, and the new capital came into being.

▶ Act naming Canberra as Australia's capital, 1908. The site was chosen partly because it was about the same distance from both Sydney and Melbourne. The site lay inside New South Wales, which surrendered it to the commonwealth. Canberra lies within Australian Capital Territory, which is not part of any state, much as Washington lies within the District of Columbia in the United States.

> 3. It is hereby determined that the Seat of Government of the Commonwealth shall be in the district of Yass-Canberra in the State of New South Wales.
>
> 4. The territory to be granted to or acquired by the Commonwealth for the Seat of Government shall contain an area not less than nine hundred square miles [1,450 square kilometers], and have access to the sea.
>
> Seat of Government Act, 1908

▲ Opening of Parliament House, Canberra, May 9, 1927. The site was chosen in 1908, and the basic design of the city was ready in 1911. There were, however, many delays. Australia's role in World War I (1914-1918) also slowed progress. The white building served as the Parliament House until 1988, when the federal Parliament moved to a new site. The building then became known as Old Parliament House.

A New Capital

3

Your Royal Highness, It is my privilege to invite you to open the door of this building, the future home of the Parliament of the Commonwealth. We recognise that this occasion marks the beginning of a new era in the history of Australia. We look back on a story of accomplishment that fills us with pride. We look forward with confidence that we will prove worthy of the great destiny that lies before us.

Stanley Bruce,
May 9, 1927

◀ Australia's Prime Minister Stanley Bruce (1883-1967) welcomes the Duke (1895-1952) and Duchess (1900-2002) of York to the opening of the Parliament Building in 1927. Bruce's words express a sense that Australia was emerging from dependence on the United Kingdom. On Dec. 11, 1931, a British act called the Statute of Westminster officially recognized that Australia, though linked to the United Kingdom and its monarch, was a fully independent nation.

▼ The Duke and Duchess of York (seated at center) open Parliament House in Canberra, May 9, 1927. The duke was the second son of King George V, who had opened the first federal Parliament in 1901 (see pages 52-53). In 1936, the Duke of York succeeded to the throne as King George VI. The duchess became Queen Elizabeth, later, Elizabeth, the Queen Mother.

4

NOW YOU KNOW

- Rivalry between Sydney and Melbourne made it hard to choose one or the other as Australia's capital.
- The solution was to build a new capital city, Canberra, in territory that was not part of any state.
- The federal Parliament opened in Canberra in 1927.

Timeline

1788 January 26	British convict ships land the first settlers at Sydney Cove, New South Wales.
1793	Free immigrants begin to arrive in New South Wales.
1803-1804	Convicts, followed by free settlers, arrive in Van Diemen's Land (now Tasmania).
1824	A convict settlement is set up in Queensland.
1825 December 3	Tasmania becomes a separate colony from New South Wales.
1829	Western Australia is founded by free settlers.
1834	The first permanent settlement of Victoria begins.
1836	South Australia is colonized by free settlers.
1839	Convicts are removed from Queensland and free settlers arrive.
1851	A gold rush begins in New South Wales and Victoria.
1851 July 1	Victoria becomes a separate colony from New South Wales.
1854 December 3	Government troops storm the rebellious miners' stockade at Eureka.
1856	New South Wales, Victoria, Tasmania, and South Australia are granted self-government.
1859 June 6	Queensland is separated from New South Wales and becomes a self-governing colony.
1861 June 30	A serious anti-Chinese riot takes place at Lambing Flat, New South Wales.
1886	The Federal Council of Australasia meets for the first time.
1889 October 24	Sir Henry Parkes's speech at Tenterfield begins the first effective campaign for federation.
1890's	Australia suffers a severe economic depression; many unions go on strike but are defeated by employers and the government.
1890 February 6-14	In Melbourne, a conference of colonial premiers selects delegates and agrees to hold a federal convention.
1890 October	Western Australia is granted self-government.
1891 March 2-April 9	The National Australasian Convention (first federal convention) meets in Sydney and agrees on a draft constitution.
1893 July 31-August 1	The People's Convention at Corowa, New South Wales, proposes new, more democratic procedures to achieve federation.
1894	South Australia gives women the vote.
1895	The colonial premiers meet in Hobart and agree to the election of delegates to a new federal convention.
1895-1896	New South Wales, Victoria, Tasmania, and South Australia pass acts to legalize the election of delegates; Western Australia decides to appoint them.
1897 March 22-March 17, 1898	Delegates from five colonies (not Queensland) meet at the second federal convention and agree on a federal constitution bill.
1898 June 3-June 4	In referendums, four colonies vote in favor of the bill, but there are not enough "Yes" votes in New South Wales.
1899	In new referendums, five colonies vote in favor of the constitution bill; Western Australia does not take part. Women gain the vote in Western Australia.
1900 July 9	The Parliament of the United Kingdom passes the Commonwealth of Australia Constitution Bill.
1900 July 31	Western Australia holds a referendum and votes in favor of federation.
1901 January 1	The Commonwealth of Australia comes into existence; Edmund Barton becomes Australia's first prime minister.
1901 March 29-30	Australia's first federal elections are held.
1901 May 9	The Duke of York opens the Commonwealth Parliament.
1902 June 12	Women are given the vote in Australia's federal elections.
1927 May 9	The Duke and Duchess of York open the first parliament in Canberra, the federal capital.
1931 December 11	A British Act of Parliament, the Statute of Westminster, officially recognizes Australia's independence.

Sources

4-5 Document 1 – Maconochie, Alexander. *Report on the State of Prison Discipline in Van Diemen's Land, etc.* London: H.M.S.O., 1938. *Google Books.* Web. 28 May 2010. Document 3 – Convicts' song. Quoted in Hughes, Robert. *The Fatal Shore.* New York: Knopf, 1986. Print.

6-7 Document 1 – British Major Robert Ross. Letter to British Under Secretary Nepean. 16 Nov. 1788. In *Historical Records of New South Wales. Vol. 1, part 2. Phillip, 1783-1792.* Sydney: Govt. Printer, 1892. *Google Books.* Web. 28 May 2010. Document 2 – Macarthur, Elizabeth. Letter to a friend. 1 Sept. 1795. In *Historical Records of New South Wales.* Vol. 2. Grose and Paterson, 1793-1795. Sydney: Govt. Printer, 1893. *Google Books.* Web. 28 May 2010.

8-9 Document 1 – Anonymous correspondent to the *Launceston Advertiser* [Tasmanian newspaper]. 1831. Quoted in Reynolds, Henry. *Why Weren't We Told?* Ringwood, Vic.: Viking, 1999. Print. Document 3 – Hobartia [pen name of an anonymous poet]. Poem published in the *Hobart Town Magazine.* 1834. Quoted in Bonwick, James. *The Lost Tasmanian Race.* London: S. Low, Marston, Searle, and Rivington, 1884. *Google Books.* Web. 28 May 2010.

10-11 Document 1 – Tolmer, Alexander. *Reminiscences of an Adventurous and Chequered Career at Home and at the Antipodes.* Vol. 2. London: Sampson Low, Marston, Searle & Rivington, 1882. *Google Books.* Web. 28 May 2010. Document 3 – Capper, John. *The Emigrant's Guide to Australia in the Eighteen Fifties.* 3rd enl. ed. 1855. Melbourne: Hawthorn Press, 1973. Print.

12-13 Document 1 – Carboni, Raffaello. *The Eureka Stockade.* Melbourne: J.P. Atkinson, 1855. *Project Gutenberg.* Web. 1 June 2010. Document 3 – *Geelong Advertiser.* 4 Dec. 1854. Quoted in "Melbourne." *Straits Times* [Singapore] 30 Jan. 1855: 6. *NewspaperSG.* Web. 1 June 2010.

14-15 Document 1 – New South Wales Constitution Act of 1855. 16 July 1855. *National Archives of Australia - Documenting Democracy.* Web. 1 June 2010. Document 3 – Denison, William. *Varieties of Vice-Regal Life.* 2 vols. London: Longmans, Green & Co., 1870. *Internet Archive.* Web. 1 June 2010.

16-17 Document 1 – Victoria Constitution Act of 1855. 16 July 1855. *National Archives of Australia - Documenting Democracy.* Web. 1 June 2010. Document 3 – "To the editor of the Perth Gazette." *Perth Gazette and Western Australian Journal.* 20 July 1833: 115. *Australian Newspapers (1803-1954).* Web. 1 June 2010.

18-19 Document 1 – "Good Morning - Happy New Year." *Moreton Bay Courier* [Brisbane, Qld.] 1 Jan. 1859: 2. *Australian Newspapers (1803-1954).* Web. 1 June 2010. Document 2 – Western Australia. Constitution Acts Amendment Act, 1899. 16 Dec. 1899. In *The Acts of Parliament of Western Australia.* Perth: Govt. Printer, 1900. *Google Books.* Web. 7 June 2010.

20-21 Document 1 – Anonymous letter to *The Argus* [Melbourne newspaper]. 5 Jan. 1859. *Australian Newspapers (1803-1954).* Web. 2 June 2010.

22-23 Document 2 – *Table Talk* [Melbourne journal]. Oct. 1891. Quoted in Welsh, Frank. *Australia: A New History of the Great Southern Land.* Woodstock, NY: Overlook Press, 2005. Print. Document 3 – "The Shearers' Dispute." *Brisbane Courier* 3 June 1891: 6. *Australian Newspapers (1803-1954).* Web. 2 June 2010.

24-25 Document 1 – "Riot at Lambing Flat." *Sydney Morning Herald* 20 July 1861: 8. *Australian Newspapers (1803-1954).* Web. 2 June 2010. Document 4 – Editorial. *Brisbane Courier* 1 March 1890: 4. *Australian Newspapers (1803-1954).* Web. 2 June 2010.

26-27 Document 1 – Angas, George Fife. Letter to Earl Grey. July 1849. Quoted in *The Centenary Companion to Australian Federation.* Ed. Helen Irving. Cambridge University Press, 1999. Print. Document 2 – "Sir Henry Parkes at Tenterfield." *Sydney Morning Herald* 25 Oct. 1889: 8. *Australian Newspapers (1803-1954).* Web. 2 June 2010. Document 3 – Edwards, Sir James Bevan. *Report by Major-General Edwards, C.B., on the Military Forces and Defences of Victoria.* . . . Melbourne: Govt. Printer, 1889. Quoted in "The Australian Defences: Major-General Edwards' Report." *Sydney Morning Herald* 15 Oct. 1889: 7. *Australian Newspapers (1803-1954).* Web. 2 June 2010.

28-29 Document 1 – Boucaut, Sir James. "Mr. Boucaut on a Policy of Progress." *Brisbane Courier* 19 Jan. 1876: 5. *Australian Newspapers (1803-1954).* Web. 2 June 2010. Document 2 – "The Federal Council." *Sydney Morning Herald* 28 Jan. 1899: 9. *Australian Newspapers (1803-1954).* Web. 2 June 2010.

30-31 Document 1 – Deakin, Alfred. *The Federal Story.* Melbourne: Robertson & Mullens, 1944. Print. Document 3 – "The Past Year." *Argus* [Melbourne] 1 Jan. 1890: 4. *Australian Newspapers (1803-1954).* Web. 2 June 2010.

32-33 Document 1 – Griffith, Sir Samuel. Speech at the Australasian Conference. 1890. In *Official Record of the Proceedings and Debates of the Australasian Federation Conference, 1890.* Melbourne: Govt. Printer, 1890. *Google Books.* Web. 2 June 2010. Document 2 – Hall, Sir John. Speech at the Australasian Conference. 1890. In *Official Record of the Proceedings and Debates of the Australasian Federation Conference, 1890.* Melbourne: Govt. Printer, 1890. *Google Books.* Web. 2 June 2010.

34-35 Document 2 – Parkes, Sir Henry. Speech at the Australasian Conference. 1890. In *Official Record of the Proceedings and Debates of the Australasian Federation Conference, 1890.* Melbourne: Govt. Printer, 1890. *Google Books.* Web. 2 June 2010. Document 3 – Editorial. *Argus* [Melbourne] 8 Feb. 1890: 8. *Australian Newspapers (1803-1954).* Web. 2 June 2010.

36-37 Document 1 – Barton, G. B., ed. *The Draft Bill to Constitute the Commonwealth of Australia.* Sydney: Govt. Printer, 1891. *Sydney Electronic Text and Image Service.* Web. 3 June 2010. Document 3 – New South Wales. *Official Report of the National Australasian Convention Debates: Sydney, 2 March to 9 April, 1891.* Sydney: G. S. Chapman, 1891. *Google Books.* Web. 3 June 2010. Document 4 – Parkes, Sir Henry. Toast at the opening banquet of the National Australasian Convention. 2 Mar. 1891. *Henry Parkes Foundation.* Web. 3 June 2010.

38-39 Document 2 – "The Corowa Federation Conference." *Sydney Morning Herald* 2 Aug. 1893: 8. *Australian Newspapers (1803-1954).* Web. 3 June 2010. Document 3 – "The Corowa Federation Conference." *Sydney Morning Herald* 2 Aug. 1893: 8. *Australian Newspapers (1803-1954).* Web. 3 June 2010.

40-41 Document 1 – Grey, Sir George. Speech at the National Australasian Convention. 8 Apr. 1891. Available in *Official Report of the National Australasian Convention Debates: Sydney, 2 March to 9 April, 1891.* Sydney: G.S. Chapman, 1891. *Google Books.* Web. 3 June 2010. Document 3 – Commonwealth of Australia Constitution Act. 9 July 1900. *Parliament of Australia.* Web. 3 June 2010.

42-43 Document 1 – Quinlan, E. E. "To the editor." *Brisbane Courier* 8 Mar. 1897: 3. *Australian Newspapers (1803-1954).* Web. 3 June 2010. Document 3 – Baker, Sir Richard. Speech at the Australian Federation Conference. 17 Mar. 1898. *ParlInfo Search.* Web. 3 June 2010.

44-45 Document 1 – "Mr. Lyne Condemns the Bill." *West Australian* [Perth, WA] 14 Apr. 1898: 5. *Australian Newspapers (1803-1954).* Web. 3 June 2010. Document 2 – Commonwealth League. "Benefits of Federation." 21 May 1898. *State Library of South Australia.* Web. 3 June 2010.

46-47 Document 2 – Deakin, Alfred. *The Federal Story.* Melbourne: Robertson & Mullens, 1944. Print.

48-49 Document 1 – Cambridge, Ada. *Thirty Years in Australia.* London: Methuen & Co., 1903. *Google Books.* Web. 3 June 2010. Document 3 – "Australia. Inauguration of the Commonwealth. An Historic Demonstration." *Argus* [Melbourne] 2 Jan. 1901: 4-6. *Australian Newspapers (1803-1954).* Web. 3 June 2010.

50-51 Document 2 – "The Federal Elections: Facts to Remember." *Advertiser* [Adelaide, SA] 27 Mar. 1901: 5. *Australian Newspapers (1803-1954).* Web. 3 June 2010. Document 3 – "Federal Candidates. 'The Mercury' List." *Mercury* [Hobart, Tas.] 28 Mar. 1901: 3. *Australian Newspapers (1803-1954).* Web. 3 June 2010.

52-53 Document 1 – Duke of York. Speech to open Australia's first Federal Parliament. 9 May 1901. In *Parliamentary Debates: Senate and House of Representatives.* Vol. 1. [Melbourne]: Govt. Printer, 1902. *Google Books.* Web. 3 June 2010. Document 2 – "Extracts from *The Age,* 10 May 1901." *Closer Look: The First Parliament of Australia.* Parliamentary Education Office, 2009. Web. 7 June 2010.

54-55 Document 2 – Braddon, Sir Edward. Speech at the Australasian Federation Conference. 17 Mar. 1898. *ParlInfo Search.* Web. 7 June 2010. Document 3 – "The Barton Cabinet. How It Ended." *Argus* [Melbourne] 25 Sept. 1903: 5. *Australian Newspapers (1803-1954).* Web. 7 June 2010.

56-57 Document 1 – Petition of the Womanhood Suffrage League of New South Wales. 24 Mar. 1897. In *Official Report of the National Australasian Convention Debates. . . . Vol. 1.* Adelaide: Govt. Printer, 1897-1898. *Google Books.* Web. 7 June 2010. Document 3 – Spence, Catherine Helen. *An Autobiography.* Adelaide: W. K. Thomas, 1910. *Project Gutenberg.* Web. 7 June 2010.

58-59 Document 1 – Australia. Seat of the Government Act 1908. 14 Dec. 1908. *National Archives of Australia - Documenting Democracy.* Web. 7 June 2010. Document 3 – Bruce, Stanley. Address at the opening of the Parliament Building. 9 May 1927. Quoted in "Path of Destiny. Inspiring Address by Mr. Bruce." *Brisbane Courier* 10 May 1927: 13. *Australian Newspapers (1803-1954).* Web. 7 June 2010.

Additional resources

Books

1901, Our Future's Past: Documenting Australia's Federation, by Raymond Evans, et al., Pan Macmillan Australia, 1997

The Commonwealth of Thieves: The Improbable Birth of Australia, by Thomas Keneally, Nan A. Talese, 2006

Edmund Barton, by Geoffrey Bolton, Allen & Unwin Academic, 2001

The Grand Old Man of Australian Politics: The Life and Times of Sir Henry Parkes, by Robert Travers, Kangaroo Press, 1993

Livewire Real Lives Sir Henry Parkes, by Teresa Llewellyn-Evans, Cambridge University Press, 1999

One Destiny!: The Federation Story—How Australia Became a Nation, by Roslyn Russell, Penguin Books, 1998

South Australia and Federation, by Peter Howell, Wakefield Press, 2002

The Story of Australia's Federation, by Leslie Horsphol, View Productions, 1985

Websites

http://www.aussieeducator.org.au/tertiary/subjects/history/australian/federation.html#feder
This page by the Aussie Educator provides many links to information and resources on Australian federation and nationalism, including journals, search engines, databases, primary documents, historical photographs and images, reference material, and other general information.

http://www.foundingdocs.gov.au/area.asp?aID=2
Documenting a Democracy, a website hosted and maintained by the National Archives of Australia, contains original documents, historical images, and timelines relating to federation and the birth of the nation.

http://www.naa.gov.au/whats-on/exhibitions/federation.aspx
The Federation Gallery, a permanent exhibition from the National Archives of Australia, brings together seven key documents in Australia's history.

http://www.nla.gov.au/exhibitions/fed-exhibition/slices/
Slices of Life 1890-1910, a site created by the National Library of Australia, explores what life was like at the time of federation.

http://setis.library.usyd.edu.au/oztexts/fed.html
The Australian Federation Full Text Database, maintained by the *Sydney Electronic Text and Image Service* at the University of Sydney, contains a full text database of federation debates and participants' writings.

Index

1890 Conference 30, 32-33, 34, 35, 40
Aborigines 4, 8-9, 18, 51, 57
Adelaide 6, 16, 21, 42
Amalgamated Shearers' Union 23
Angas, George Fife 26
Angas, George French 10
Anglo-Boer War 46, 52
Anti-Chinese riots 24-25
Australasian Federation League 39
Australian Labor Party 23, 24, 50
Australian Natives' Association 39

Baker, Sir Richard 43
Ballarat 12, 13
Banks 22, 23
Barton, Sir Edmund 38, 39, 42, 47, 50, 51, 53, 54-55
Bathurst 10, 38, 39
Bathurst People's Convention 38, 39
Black, George 12
Boucaut, James 28
Braddon, Sir Edward 29, 43, 54
Brisbane 6, 18, 19
Britain see United Kingdom
British Empire 24, 46
Bruce, Stanley 59

Cablegram communications 20, 52
Cambridge, Ada 48
Canberra 58, 59
Capitals
  federal 58-59
  state 6, 7, 14, 16, 18, 19, 49
Capper, John 11
Cerberus (battleship) 27
Chain gangs 4
Chamberlain, Joseph 46
Chanter, John 39
Children 15, 17
Cities 4, 7, 10, 20, 48, 49, 58-59
Clark, Andrew Inglis 33, 36
Climate 6, 17, 18
Cockburn, John Alexander 33
Commonwealth of Australia 30, 36, 41, 44, 45, 46, 47, 48, 49
Commonwealth of Australia Constitutional Act 44, 46, 47, 54
Commonwealth Bill see Commonwealth of Australia Constitutional Act

Constitutions
  federal 32, 34, 35, 36, 37, 38, 40, 42, 43, 44, 47, 48, 54, 56
  New South Wales 14
  U.S. 34, 35
  Victoria 16
  Western Australia 18
Convicts 4, 5, 6, 14, 15, 16, 18, 21
Cook, James 4
Corowa People's Convention 38, 39
Cotton, H. 31, 56

Darwin 21
Deakin, Alfred 30, 33, 46, 51
Defense 26, 27, 28, 32
Denison, Sir William 15
Depression, economic 22-23, 36, 38
Dickson, James Robert 29, 47

Economy 4, 10, 14, 16, 18, 20, 22-23, 36, 38
Edward VII, King 52, 53
Edwards, James Bevan 27
Eight-Hour Day Movement 22
Elections
  convention delegates 38, 42, 57
  federal 50-51, 56
Enabling act 42
Eureka Stockade 12-13

Farming 5, 6, 14, 18, 20
  sheep raising 6, 14, 20
Federal Conventions
  First (1891) 32, 34, 36-37, 40
  Second (1897-1898) 38, 42-43, 54, 56, 57
Federal Council 28-29, 31
Federal Leagues 38
Fiji 28
Flag, Eureka 13
Foreign policy 16, 27, 46
Forrest, John 29, 43
Free Trade Party 50, 51

Geeveston Forest 21
Gillies, Duncan 33
Gold mining 10, 11, 18, 20, 24
Gold Rush 10-11, 12, 14, 16, 24, 45
Grey, Henry George 26
Grey, Sir George 40

Griffith, Sir Samuel 32, 36, 55

Hall, Sir John 32, 33
Hargreaves, Edward 11
Hebblethwaite, James 15
High Court of Australia 54, 55
Hobart 4, 6, 14, 15, 38, 42
Hopetoun, Lord (governor general) 48, 52, 53
House of Representatives 36, 48, 51

Immigrants 6, 8, 11, 16, 17, 24, 25
  see also Settlers

Jenkins, G. H. 33

Kingston, Charles 42, 43, 47

Labor Party see Australian Labor Party
Lalor, Peter 12
Lambing Flat riots 24-25
Land rights, Aboriginal 8
Legislative Assemblies
  New South Wales 14
  Queensland 19
  South Australia 17
  Victoria 16
Legislative Council, Victoria 16
Lister, John 10
Logging 21
Lyne, William 44

Macarthur, Elizabeth 6
Macarthur, John 6
Maconochie, Alexander 4
McMillan, William 33
Melbourne 6, 16, 20, 22, 23, 30, 32, 38, 42, 43, 49, 52, 54, 55, 58
Miners 12, 13, 24

National Australasian Convention (First Federal Convention, 1891) 32, 34, 36-37, 40
Nationalism 24-25, 26
Nelson, Sir Hugh 42
New South Wales 4, 6, 7, 10, 14, 16, 18, 20, 24, 26, 28, 30, 31, 33, 36, 37, 38, 39, 41, 42, 43, 44, 45, 49, 54, 56, 58
New Woman 57

63

Index

New Zealand 28, 32, 33, 36, 40-41

O'Connor, Richard 55
Ophir 10

Parkes, Sir Henry 26, 27, 30-31, 32, 33, 35, 36, 37
Parliament House, Canberra 58, 59
Parliaments 35
   federal 35, 37, 52-53, 56, 57, 58, 59
   New South Wales 54
   opening of 52-53
   Victoria 12, 16
Parramatta 6, 7
People's Conventions 38-39
Perth 6, 49
Phillip, Arthur 7
Playford, Thomas 33
Police 10, 12, 15, 23
Population 20, 21, 26, 32, 36, 44
   Aboriginal 9
   European 4, 6, 10, 15, 16, 17, 18, 19
Prospectors 10, 11
Protectionist Party 50

Queensland 18-19, 29, 42, 44
Quick, John 38

Racism 18
Railroads 20, 21, 26

Referendums 38, 42, 44-45, 56
Reid, George 39, 43, 50
Roberts, Tom 53
Ross, Major Robert 6
Russell, William 33

Schools 15
Senate 36, 43, 44, 48
Settlements 4, 6, 7, 14, 16, 17
Settlers
   Aborigines 4, 8
   European 4, 5, 6, 8-9, 14
   free 5, 6-7, 14, 16, 18
Shaw, James 17
South Australia 10, 14, 16-17, 18, 26, 28, 33, 41, 42, 43, 44, 51, 56, 57
Southern Cross 13, 24
Spence, Catherine Helen 57
Statute of Westminster 59
Strikes 23
Strutt, William 16
Suffrage movement 56, 57
Sydney 4, 6, 7, 18, 36, 42, 48, 49, 54, 58
Sydney Cove 4, 6

Tariffs 26, 37, 40, 50
Tasmania 4, 5, 8, 9, 14, 15, 21, 29, 33, 41, 42, 43, 44, 51, 54
Tiffin, Charles 19
Tolmer, Alexander 10

Trade 37, 44, 50, 51
Trade unions 22, 23, 24
Transportation of convicts 4
Turner, Sir George 28, 29, 43

Unemployment 22
United Kingdom 4, 5, 6, 8, 16, 18, 26, 28, 35, 36, 41, 46-47, 52, 59
United States 20, 26, 34, 35, 58

Van Diemen's Land *see* Tasmania
Victoria 10, 12, 14, 16, 20, 27, 28, 29, 30, 31, 33, 37, 41, 42, 43, 44
Victoria, Queen 46, 47, 52, 53
Voting rights 14, 18, 40, 43, 51, 56-57

Wakefield, Edward Gibbon 17
Western Australia 18, 29, 41, 42, 43, 44, 45, 49, 51, 56
White Australia policy 18, 24
Womanhood Suffrage League 56
Women 11, 18, 51, 56-57
Working conditions 25

Yagan 8
York, Duke of (1865-1936) 46, 52, 53
York, Duke of (1895-1952) 59

Zig Zag Railway 20

Acknowledgments

ACT Government & Assembly Library: 31; **Art Archive:** 7, 16; **Art Gallery of Ballarat:** 13; **Bathurst Library, New South Wales:** 39; **Bridgeman Art Library:** 10, 36; **Corbis:** 21 (Cannon Collection/Australian Picture Library), 46, 54; **Department of Parliamentary Services, Canberra, A.C.T.:** 47, 53; **Getty Images:** 14 (Hulton Archive), 48; **James Shaw,** *The South Australian Parliament: The House of Assembly,* South Australian Government Grant 1959, Art Gallery of South Australia, Adelaide: 17; **Lambing Flat Folk Museum/Young Historical Society:** 24; **Mary Evans Picture Library:** 12, 20, 33, 49, 57; **Museum of HMAS** *Cerberus***:** 27; **National Archives of Australia** (A1200 2/1918/20A/2)**:** 25; **National Archives and Records Administration,** 34; **National Library of Australia:** 8, 9, 29, 38, 55, 56; **National Museum of Australia:** 5 (Dean McNicoll), 11 (George Serras), 43 (Matt Kelso); **State Library of New South Wales:** 45, 50; **State Library of Queensland** (negative no. 4005)**:** 19; **State Library of South Australia:** 42, 47; **State Library of Western Australia, the Battye Library** (52566P)**:** 45; **Topfoto:** 1, 4, 21, 22, 23, 30, 40, 41, 58, 59; **W. L. Crowther Library:** 15.

Cover main image: **Shutterstock**; inset image: **Topfoto**